THESE STRANGE GERMAN WAYS

Fourteenth Edition

Published by Atlantik-Brücke e. V.
Sanderskoppel 15, 2000 Hamburg 65, Federal Republic of Germany

Picture Series and Cover by Jörn
Printed in Germany by SEEHAFEN-VERLAG, Hamburg
Fourteenth Edition, 1980

A Word About This Booklet

This booklet is published by Atlantik-Brücke (Atlantic Bridge), a private group of German citizens who desire to further international, and particularly, German-American understanding.

The picture series on German customs and many of the articles first appeared in THE BRIDGE, a monthly paper which for more than 13 years was published by Atlantik-Brücke for American servicemen stationed in Germany. Although, therefore, much of the material was written and presented primarily with Americans in mind, it is hoped that the booklet may be useful and informative for any interested English-speaking person.

We would like to thank all those who have contributed to this booklet with valuable tips and suggestions. Particular mention should be made of Adolph Schalk, an American writer and newspaperman who created THE BRIDGE and began the series on "These Strange German Ways;" Carolyn Campbell, editorial assistant for several years; Jürgen Brandes; Ruth M. Irvin; Robert C. Larson; Victor Baras; Joetta Moltmann; and Marian Tursich.

In the 13 editions since 1963, when this booklet first appeared, there have been many revisions of its contents. Customs have been changing fast along with the West Germans' way of life, which has come to resemble more and more the life style of other western industrial societies. Sometimes we even wondered if in the long run there would be enough "Strange" German ways left to warrant the publication of this book! But the present 14th edition proves that such doubts are unfounded: again many details had to be revised, and many new features were added to explain Germany to Americans and to other English-speaking people. — On the surface, the differences do not seem to be very great anymore; but it is often the little misunderstandings that lead to irritations, disappointments, or even "culture shock." We hope that this little book will help to make things a bit easier.

Great care has been taken to ensure that all facts and figures given are correct and up to date. Nevertheless, errors may still have crept in and some details may become obsolete after printing. We would appreciate it if inaccuracies, errors, or discrepancies were brought to our attention for revision in the next edition.

Walter Stahl
Executive Vice President, Atlantik-Brücke

Irmgard Burmeister
Editor

Table of Contents

The Social Courtesies

Most Americans in Germany know what "Auf Wiedersehen" means: good-bye. But what is "Tschüss?" And "Grüss Gott?" And what do the Germans say for "thank you," or for "excuse me?" — Even if you don't speak the language, knowing a few words of greeting, of thanks, of apology, will make you feel so much better in the foreign surroundings. And knowing some basic differences in the social courtesies — when to shake hands, when to use first names, how to introduce people — can make all the difference.

Try it and see!

May I Introduce You?

Darf ich bekannt machen?

What do you say when introducing people to each other in Germany? Say "Darf ich bekannt machen?" or "Darf ich vorstellen? — Herr Meier — Frau Schmidt." The two shake hands, smile and say "Guten Abend (Guten Tag), Herr/Frau..." to each other. A friendly nod of the head when shaking hands would do, too. You may also say "Freut mich sehr" or "sehr angenehm" (corresponding to the American "Very glad to meet you") on such occasions, but these phrases are regarded as somewhat old-fashioned by many Germans and not used much anymore.

As a rule, Germans will prefer being introduced to a stranger by a third person instead of introducing themselves. However, if the circumstances call for it, it is perfectly all right to introduce oneself. Just say your last name: "Schmidt." A man asking a woman he has not met before for a dance displays good manners if he first introduces himself to her. In formal German introductions, the name of the man or, if it concerns two men or two women, the name of the younger or lower ranking person is said first!

Americans, who are used to saying "How do you do" or "how are you" when being introduced, may be tempted to say "Wie geht es Ihnen?" when being introduced to a German. This is not customary, however. "Wie geht es Ihnen?" is a greeting for someone you already know, and when using it be prepared to get a detailed answer. Even the more casual "Wie geht's?" may be understood as an inquiry rather than a polite greeting. "Danke, gut!" (thank you, fine) would be the normal answer, though.

Guten Tag! Auf Wiedersehen!

"Hello" or "Hi" have become almost international greetings these days, and many Germans will use them when dealing with Americans. Their own language does not know such short, informal greetings, although you do hear "Hallo" among young people and children.

The normal German greeting is "Guten Tag" (Guten Abend, Guten Morgen) and in Southern Germany, "Grüss Gott." Often, people just mumble "n' Tag," "n' Abend," or "Morgen!"

"(Auf) Wiedersehen" means good-bye. "Tschüss" (originating, by the way, from the french "A Dieu") is a very casual form of "Wiedersehen." It comes closest to the American "See you!" or "So long!"

If a German says "Bis bald!" (until soon) or "Bis dann!" (until then), he usually has a specific time in mind, something he has just talked about. Actually, there is no need for a German to express his hope to see the other person again, as "Auf Wiedersehen" means exactly that.

Guten Tag, Guten Morgen, Grüß Gott!

Auf Wiedersehen!

Germans also use these greetings when entering or leaving a shop.

Who Shakes Whose Hand?

Germans have a reputation as great hand-shakers. They used to pump each others' hands not only when being introduced but also as a normal part of everyday greetings, meaning little more than saying hello.

This, as so many features of a less hectic way of life, has changed rapidly in the last ten or twenty years. More and more Germans shake hands now only when meeting strangers, when seeing friends or relatives after a prolonged absence, or when congratulating. The practice now varies so much in all regions and population groups that it is impossible to give a strict rule for all occasions. When in doubt whether a handshake is in place, the foreigner would be better off leaving it and waiting for the German to make the first move.

According to formal convention, it is the senior or the lady who offers the hand first, but this rule, too, is increasingly being ignored. It is considered very bad manners, however, to leave one hand in the pocket when shaking hands.

At a small German party (not at a big cocktail party, of course) everybody will greet everybody else he knows with a handshake, beginning with the host and hostess. A stranger normally waits until the host makes the introductions. A woman need not rise when greeting a man or another woman, unless the other woman is considerably older or a very distinguished person. A man should rise when a woman enters the room for the first time.

When meeting acquaintances in the street, in shops or elsewhere in public, Germans usually shake hands only if they intend to stop and have a little chat.

Sometimes, when two couples greet each other, one can watch a funny little scene: they all stretch out their hands at once and, noticing this, suddenly draw them back before contact, smiling a little wryly. The reason for this is the superstition that one should never shake hands crosswise, as this surely will bring bad luck. The solution to the problem is again, "ladies first!"

Perhaps to make up for less handshaking, Americans do a lot more kissing when greeting each other than Germans. Of late, however, a peck on the cheek among friends is seen more often in Germany than before.

The Hand Kiss

Americans are often startled when witnessing for the first time an old formality of German society — the hand kiss. A survey revealed that about 40% of the German women like this custom, but 80% of the German men don't! By the way: the hand is not actually kissed — a paper-thin sheet of air must remain between the hand and lips. A hand kiss takes place only indoors, never in the street.

And here's another warning to foreign visitors: to perform a hand kiss elegantly takes a certain amount of practice, and it is really only done in society circles (and among those who long to belong...).

Too Little Is Better Than Too Much!

Only at small parties, all people shake hands, not at large affairs.

No need to shake hands in the street — and few German men wear hats nowadays.

The hand kiss — still a formality of German society, but only indoors.

More Little Courtesies

Knicks

Compliment

Wedding Ring or Not?

Another custom that is on the way out: only few German mothers still teach their little daughters to courtsey ("einen Knicks machen") when greeting adults. If little boys bow to adults, this is called "einen Diener machen" (Diener — servant), but this, too, has become a very rare sight.

Don't be surprised if a German girl does not automatically say "thank you" when you have paid her a compliment. She may say "danke schön," but this is not a standard answer as it would be in the States. The German girl's answer is left more or less up to her imagination. In any case, she likes to get a compliment just as much as the American girl does.

In spite of women's lib and ever more young couples living together without marriage, German wives — contrary to their husbands — still prefer to show their marital status: According to a survey made a few years ago, only half of all married men but seven out of eight married women in Germany wear their wedding ring.

Traditionally, Germans wear their wedding ring on the right hand and the engagement ring on the left hand (the engagement ring is usually the same plain gold band that later serves as the wedding ring). Nowadays, however, many men and women wear the wedding ring on the left hand, and only half of all engaged people in Germany said they wear an engagement ring at all. Still others wear a wedding ring without being married.

A confusing picture — but it shows clearly the degree to which old-established social rules and attitudes are in flux in Germany at the present time.

Bitte, danke, Verzeihung

If a German gives a person something — or if he picks something up for another person, holds the door open, etc. — he usually says "Bitte" (Bitte sehr, Bitte schön). On receiving something from another person, one will say "Danke" (Danke sehr, Danke schön). Upon this, an American would answer "you're welcome." The German answer to "Danke" is "Bitte," sometimes also: "nichts zu danken" or "keine Ursache" (don't mention it).

If you step on somebody's foot, what do you say to express that you are sorry? You may say "Verzeihung" (Verzeihen Sie, bitte; Entschuldigung; Entschuldigen Sie, bitte). The victim will answer "Bitte sehr" or a similar Bitte phrase, and — if he's a very polite man — even lift his hat.

What do you say if you wish to make your way through a crowd, especially in a bus, streetcar, etc.? The most polite way is to ask "Gestatten Sie, bitte?" but you will also often simply hear "Verzeihung," (Entschuldigung, entschuldigen Sie), "steigen Sie auch aus?" (Are you also getting out?)

Bitte schön! — Danke schön!

"Entschuldigen Sie, bitte!"

It's easy in this case (ladies first), but if two men or two women want to go through a door, they often make quite a polite fuss over who should go first: "nach Ihnen!" (after you).

Frau or Fräulein?

**Adult women are addressed with "Frau"
married or not.**

A letter to "Frau Helga Müller."

In Germany, unmarried adult women now-adays are called "Frau" instead of "Fräu-lein." The latter is now only used for very young unmarried girls. Also all women artists, actresses, or anyone who is distin-guished in any way, and who in America would be addressed with "Miss," would be called "Frau" in German.

In postal addresses, "Frau" is used almost exclusively now.

Married women are not addressed with their husband's first name — their own first name is used. Thus, it is not "Frau Hans Müller" but "Frau Helga Müller." The American method is used only rarely.

Widowed women keep their married name, while divorced women are free to use their maiden name again.

Since 1976, partners in marriage may also chose the woman's name for the family — but only few couples do so.

Gnädige Frau — Ihre Gattin — mein Mann

How would the hotel reception clerk address the female guest? Most probably with "Gnädige Frau." This is the most polite form of addressing a woman in Germany, comparable in a way to "Madam" in English, although "Gnädige Frau" is more formal.

Suppose two men know each other only slightly and meet in the train by accident. In asking how the other's wife is doing, they have three grades of formality to choose from: "Wie geht es Ihrer Frau"(normal, but a bit informal), "... Ihrer Gattin" (very polite), "Ihrer Frau Gemahlin" (very formal).

Speaking of her husband, a woman uses the term "mein Mann." Germans always say "mein Mann" or "meine Frau," no matter how formal the occasion may be. Never would Frau Schmidt speak of her husband as "Herr Schmidt" or vice versa.

More Than Just a Different Custom:

The Ticklish Business of "Sie" and "Du"

"Typical German stiffness," Americans may think when they hear how some Germans say "Sie" and "Herr" to each other even after several years of acquaintance.

It is true that the "Du" (and first name) is the general intimate form and the "Sie" (and family name) the more formal mode of addressing a person, but to a German "Herr Müller" and "Sie" does not sound as formal as "Mr. Miller" sounds to an American. On the other hand, calling a German by his first name and "Du" can denote a much greater intimacy than calling an American by his first name.

It depends very much on the social environment. For instance, colleagues in an office may call each other by the family name and "Sie" for years, and yet the atmosphere can be very cordial and informal. Generally, "Sie" is used among white-collar employees, professional people and civil servants, while manual workers, lower echelon and very young employees almost always will say "Du" to each other (but "Sie" to the boss; as a rule the boss will also use "Sie" and the family name in talking to his workers). In small communities, most people will say "Du" to each other. So do military comrades (but in dealings between officers and servicemen, the "Sie" form will be used). Also members of the Social Democratic Party and trade unionists traditionally use "Du" with one another. "Du" in all these cases connotes a certain feeling of solidarity.

A survey revealed that about one quarter of all adult Germans quickly change to "Du" after having made friends, but more than 40 % wait for quite some time. Men use "Du" twice as often with friends as women do. "Du" is always used within the family and with children up to mid-adolescence.

Most young people up to their mid-twenties, too, normally use the "Du" among each other. Students will say "Sie" to their teachers and professors and vice versa, unless the professors are exceptionally progressive-minded and insist on "Du."

Always Use "Sie" First

The foreigner is always well advised to use "Sie" (and family name) first and then play it by ear. Usually it is the older person who suggests the switch to "Du."

If two Germans decide to associate on a "Du" basis, they may even celebrate the occasion by way of "Brüderschaft trinken" (drink to brotherhood): wine or beer glass in hand, the two people hook arms and each sips from his own glass. Then they shake hands and kiss lightly if women, and announce their first name, such as "ich heisse Monika." Like so many old customs, however, this "Brüderschaft" ceremony, too, is regarded as somewhat ridiculous by the younger generation.

It was the younger set that — beginning with the student movement of the late 1960s — has helped "Du" to make much progress in recent years. After a while, however, every young generation turns into a middle-aged generation, and then it often returns to the time-honored convention.

Actually, we touch here upon a deep difference between the attitudes and conventions of Germans /Europeans and Americans, the result of quite different social traditions: While Americans, in becoming acquainted, automatically try to create a relaxed, informal atmosphere, Germans (and most other Europeans, too, for that matter) react with a kind of polite formality. Germans accept the distance between strangers as a normal fact of life, and the "Sie" means just that. No offense meant!

The Ticklish Business of "Sie" and "Du"

All members of a family say "Du" to each other. Children are always addressed with "Du," until mid-adolescence.

Colleagues in the professions and office workers mostly say "Sie," while blue-collar workers and military comrades say "Du" to each other.

In German social life, "Du" and first name usage connotes a very close, intimate friendship. — Young people, however, are quick at making "Du" friends.

The Man Should Walk on the Left Side

Many young people in Germany will tell you that it does not matter who should walk on the left: the man or the woman. Many of the older ones, however — and perhaps just the girl you wish to impress with your good manners! — will note it immediately if the foreign visitor makes an effort to adapt to German custom.

As a basic rule, a man walks on the left side of a woman in Germany — in the streets and everywhere. The place on the right is always the "place of honor," so to speak. Therefore, also a young girl would walk on the left side of an old lady, for instance.

When two men and one woman are walking together, the woman should walk in the middle. If a man walks with two women, he would normally also stay in the middle, so as to devote equal attention to both.

Keep to the Side of the Traffic

Considerate men do not follow this rule, however, when walking in a very narrow street or wherever traffic is so heavy that it might disturb or even endanger the woman at his side. Then, the man keeps to the side where the traffic is, like in the States.

Why this rule of keeping to the left? Until now, we have heard two explanations for that custom. The first one sounds very romantic. It says that the escort always wanted to be close to the side where the lady's heart was. The second explanation gives a more practical reason, although it is somewhat romantic, too, because it goes back to the times of the medieval knights. Since a knight used to have his sword on his left, this explanation says, it was natural for the woman to go on the other side, where the sword could not disturb her.

The Man Should Walk on the Left Side

Normally the escort keeps to the left side in Germany

"Left is where the heart is"

The "sword theory"

Guten Morgen, Herr Professor!

A Few Words About German Titles

Although titles are certainly no longer so important in Germany as they used to be, it is still true that more than in other Western countries a person's social prestige is determined by his professional standing and title.

There are variations, of course. In a big city, for instance, a teacher is not such a highly honored personality as in a small village, where he may still be addressed as "Herr Lehrer." Also, younger people are on the whole much less title-conscious than those who grew up in Kaiser Wilhelm's time. And the North Germans use fewer titles than the South Germans. But the stranger who wants to get along with the people is well-advised if he tries to adapt to the established local usage, although it may perhaps seem a little ridiculous at times.

"Herr Doktor Meier"

All German forms of address, with only a very few exceptions, begin with "Herr" or "Frau," followed by either the title and/or the family name. The holders of a German doctor's degree — not only medical doctors — are addressed as "Herr Doktor So-and-So." The family name often is left out when addressing doctors of medicine. A university professor is called "Herr Professor," with or without the family name. (Some younger doctors or professors do not use their titles however.) Never will two titles be used at the same time (like: Herr Professor Doktor, or Herr Doktor Präsident), but if a person holds several titles, the higher one is used in speaking to him. In addressing a letter one would write: "Herrn Prof. Dr. Hans Meier," but the salutation would be: "Sehr verehrter Herr Professor!" or "Sehr verehrter Herr Professor Meier!"

The mayor of a town is called "Herr Bürgermeister." Judges are addressed as "Herr Richter." Common names for clergy are "Herr Pfarrer" or "Herr Pastor," for Catholic clergy also "Hochwürden."

A "Minister" is not a clergyman in Germany, but a government department head.

With government officials, too, the rank or title is preceded by "Herr" (or "Frau"), as e.g. Herr Minister, Herr Staatssekretär, Herr Ministerpräsident, Herr Botschafter, etc. The three highest-ranking personalities in the federal German government are addressed as Herr Bundespräsident (foreigners say Eure Exzellenz), Herr Bundestagspräsident and Herr Bundeskanzler.

The members of the Bundestag are officially called "Herr Abgeordneter," otherwise simply "Herr So-and-So."

In the military, the "Herr" is added to the rank: "Herr General", "Herr Oberstleutnant," "Herr Major," "Herr Hauptmann;" of late, also the lowest grades below the non-commissioned officer are addressed this way: "Herr Gefreiter."

"Herr Kollege"

An educated German never introduces himself with his title or rank, but rather he will say only his family name. Also, persons of equal rank do not use their titles when talking with one another. Two professors or two doctors will say "Herr So-and-So" to each other, or "Herr Kollege," if they belong to the same profession.

Women have it relatively easy in German protocol. They need not address men with their professional titles when meeting them socially, unless the difference in social standing or age is very great. Whether they should use the titles in professional life depends very much on the given circumstances.

A woman with an academic degree is adressed as "Frau Doktor So-and-So" or "Frau Professor." It is not correct — although you will hear it sometimes — to address a married woman with her husband's title (such as "Frau Direktor" or "Frau Präsident.") "Gnädige Frau," which is roughly equivalent to the English "Madam," is always correct when dealing with women of social status. Women themselves, however, will only use this form of address when the difference in status is very great.

Nobility

It is impossible in this short space also to explain all the intricate ranks of German nobility. One should perhaps know that the prefix "von" as well as designations such as "Freiherr" and "Graf" do not denote social ranks anymore but are to be considered as parts of the name. The correct form of address is generally "Herr (or Frau) von So-and-So," while counts are called "Graf (or Gräfin) So-and-So," not "Herr Graf."

All this may sound complicated, but actually it is not that bad. After all, one does not meet a count or a chancellor every day, and a foreigner will readily be excused if he makes a mistake.

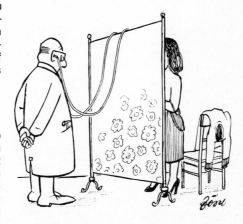

"I'm afraid I am a little prudish, Herr Doktor...!"

Meeting, Visiting and Living with Germans

Americans have often asked us why Germans, particularly of the middle and older generations, are so "formal" when meeting people and inviting friends. Customs do differ in this respect, and the reason is to be found in the different historical background.

They Stayed Where They Were

While America is a nation of immigrants, Germany is not. In order to survive in the foreign surroundings, immigrants to the U.S. had to develop forms of behavior that allowed them to quickly get acquainted with all kinds of strangers from vastly different ethnic and cultural backgrounds. The Germans and all other Europeans have never gone through this experience of amalgamation. They more or less stayed where they were — in a given region, with a given set of traditions and manners that allowed them to get along with a relatively close circle of neighbors, co-workers, and friends. As a result, their language and customs did not develop the forms that help Americans to overcome the distance between strangers so easily and quickly.

Even today, Germans are not used to moving about as much as Americans do. A recent survey showed that even upon losing their jobs, many Germans would rather put up with a very long commuting distance (58%) or learn another trade (41%) than change their place of residence (a German buys a house only once)! While in America about one fifth of the population moves every year, the majority of Germans still spend their whole life in the same place or at least in the same region where they were born and grew up, within a circle of people they have known for a long time.

When meeting a stranger or a foreigner, the average German will be friendly but he will not make a special effort to overcome the distance and the feeling of strangeness. Don't mistake this behavior as coldness or lack of good will; the distance is seen as the most natural thing in the world, not as a barrier that must be overcome as quickly as possible.

Being situated in the center of Europe, Germany has often in the course of the centuries had foreign visitors — from missionaries to occupation troops, merchants, migrant workers, and tourists. They are nothing uncommon, therefore,

Invitation to a German Home

and few people are likely to approach you simply because you are from another country. On the contrary: on the part of some Germans (certain landlords, for instance) you may even hit upon open refusal and distrust of **all** "Ausländer." Don't generalize such experiences, but remember:

Friendships Take Time

If you wish to establish social contacts with Germans, the initiative must come from your side. But don't be "pushy." Feel your way and be prepared to wait for a personal friendship to develop. The best way is probably to join a German-American Club or a German hobby club — sports club, stamp collectors club, or to whatever your interests may lead you.

Most Germans live in a rather narrow, close network of social relationships which are determined by tradition and custom as well as by the individual's education and job status. Home life is of greatest significance, both as a shelter from the turmoils and stress of the outside world and as an expression of one's own private standing. Most German housewives take great pride in the way their home is equipped and kept up — sometimes even at the cost of cultivating social contacts.

All this means, of course, that not only for foreigners but also for Germans who have to move to another location it may become quite difficult to make new friends.

If you have been formally invited to a private German home you may consider it as a special gesture of friendship. You may well expect that your visit has been carefully prepared for: the house will be spick and span, "Kuchen" may have been baked

for coffee or a good dinner may have been cooked, and the family will be dressed up for the occasion.

If you are invited for coffee or a meal, come on time and bring along a little bouquet of flowers for the hostess. Usually an uneven number of five or seven — according to size — is given. When presenting the flowers, do not forget that one is supposed to remove the wrapping before handing them to the hostess. (And be careful with red roses — they can be poison ivy if given to the wrong person at the wrong time, because they are usually offered by a lover to his sweetheart.)

At a large party with many guests, flowers are often not brought along but sent before the party or the next day, together with a short note. A "bread-and-butter-letter" is not necessary in Germany if you have brought or sent flowers. After a nice party, the wife of the invited couple may call the hostess and say a few words of thanks.

Bring Along a Little Bouquet of Flowers

Casual visits are rare, private invitations a special gesture of friendship.

Take off the wrapping of the flowers before presenting them.

Red roses mean something special (See page 19).

Flowers and Plants in the Windows

Most German housewives take great pride in the looks of their windows. You see fancifully tucked-up curtains everywhere and flowers and potted plants in the windows of most every house. Contrary to the United States, fly screening is rarely seen here, but there are more curtains and stores behind the windows.

The abundance of flowers and plants in the windows delights most visitors to Germany. A recent survey showed that each German family has an average of 12 potted plants, thus following Denmark (with 15 plants) in the absolute world record. No less than 9,000 German flower shops belong to the international Fleurop organization. The average German household spends about DM 100 annually on flowers.

You will also see many public buildings, streets and parks decorated with flowers in the summer time.

An abundance of plants in the windows and on the balconies.

No Long Cocktail Hour Before Dinner!

Coming much too late makes a bad impression in Germany.

"Entschuldigen Sie bitte, dass ich so spät komme, aber…"

Most Germans consider punctuality a great virtue, also in private appointments. If you have been invited for dinner in Germany, you are expected to arrive on time. Do not come earlier, but also not later than ten or 15 minutes (naturally, this does not apply to buffets or receptions). The long cocktail hour before dinner is not known in Germany.

What do you say if you are late anyhow? Say: "Entschuldigen Sie bitte, dass ich so spät komme" or "dass ich mich verspätet habe" or "dass ich Sie warten liess, aber…" (please excuse me for coming so late, or: for being late, or: for letting you wait, but…)

Some standard excuses:

Ich wurde aufgehalten (I was held up)

Der Verkehr war so dicht, ich kam nicht durch
(The traffic was so dense, I did not get through)

Ich fand keinen Parkplatz
(I could not find a parking space)

Please, Help Yourself!

„Nehmen Sie Sahne und Zucker zum Kaffee?" (Do you take cream and sugar with your coffee?) the hostess may ask. The guest either accepts ("Ja, danke") or says "Nur Sahne, bitte" (only cream, please) or explains that he prefers his coffee black: "Nein, danke, ich trinke ihn (den Kaffee) schwarz!"

Asking someone to hand you the sugar, you may say: "Würden Sie mir bitte den Zucker reichen?" In handing it over, the other person will say "Bitte sehr!" and you thank him or her with "Danke sehr!" or "Danke schön!" — "Please, help yourself" would be "Bitte, bedienen Sie sich!" in German.

"Bitte, möchten Sie (nehmen Sie) noch ein Stück Kuchen?" (Would you like to have — will you take — another piece of cake?) More formal would be: "Darf ich Ihnen noch ein Stück Kuchen geben?" (May I give you...) — "Ja, bitte!" or "Nein, danke!" "Danke" or "Ich danke" alone may also mean "No, thank you."

Eating and Drinking Manners

One of the things that startles most Americans newly arrived in Germany is the way the Germans eat. Whenever they eat something that requires cutting, they hold the fork in the left hand and the knife in the right, keeping them this way throughout the meal. The knife is also used to push the food onto the fork. If a knife is not needed, the left hand is placed on the table beside the plate, not in the lap.

Most Germans do not cut potatoes with a knife, but use the fork instead. This is a relic from the times when blades were not yet made of stainless steel. Nor is cooked fish cut with a knife, but either with a special fish knife or with a fork.

Seldom will you see a German drink plain water with his meals, but mostly beer or wine.

Toasting at a Formal Dinner Party

In Germany nobody drinks at a dinner party before the host has drunk. The host first tests the wine for temperature and then fills (or has filled) the glasses of his guests, his own last. But he is the first to drink, raising his glass to the woman on his right and then toasting the health of the group. Thereafter, people may drink as they see fit. The most accepted toast is "Zum Wohl!" (to your health). The host usually will add some words of greeting and good wishes. "Prost" comes closest to "cheers."

Toasting among the guests is an old-established German custom. This also can be done from a certain distance, provided one catches the eye of the person one intends to honor. The toaster then nods towards the person he wants to toast, who smiles back, then sips his wine and receives a nod and a sip in turn. Both glasses are then raised again and finally lowered at the same time. The person of higher rank initiates the toast towards his inferior, who is expected to return the toast a little later; between a man and a woman, it is always the man who makes the overture.

As a rule, Germans clink their glasses only when wishing each other luck or when celebrating some special event as a birthday or wedding. Only glasses with wine or champagne are clinked together, beer sometimes (in Bavaria), brandy never.

Seating —

In Germany, a guest of honor is seated to the left of the hostess, if it's a man, and to the right of the host, if it's a woman.

— and Sneezing:

Contrary to the U. S., in Germany it is not considered bad manners if you blow your nose at the dinner table — as long as it's done in a discreet way!

Eating and Drinking Manners

Germans keep the fork in the left hand throughout the meal, and the knife in the right. If the left hand is not needed, it is placed on the table beside the plate.

At a German dinner party, the host drinks first, raising his glass to the health of his guests.

My Home Is My Castle

It must be the cool climate and the long, dark winters that make a cozy home so all-important for the Germans. "Die Wohnung" (dwelling, living place) ranks highest above all other goods, even above the car and vacation trips. Only their health, family and job are closer to the Germans' heart, opinion pollsters have found out. Nine out of ten Germans would like to live in their own apartment or house, but only every third family has reached that goal; two thirds live in rented apartments.

Privacy is more important here than in the U.S. with its "pioneer neighborliness." When moving into a new community, Germans usually do not make special efforts to meet their new neighbors. They may make a short visit to the people living next door, but this is not automatically expected of them. It is also not customary that the oldtimers come to welcome the newcomers. Getting to know one's neighbors is more or less left to chance. Germans also build more fences than Americans. There are exceptions in modern housing settlements, but usually every house has a fenced-in front yard, and if there is a back yard, this will be fenced-off, too.

Another contrast to the U.S.: Germans tend to close their office doors rather than leave them open. This is also true for private homes. Before entering, knock at the door, even if it's "public." "Herein" means "come in."

Saving Energy, Too

In addition to the cherished privacy, there is another, more practical reason for the closing of doors: heating. Many German homes do not yet have central heating and even where that is the case the tendency is to turn up the heat just in the living room, leaving the rest of the house cooler. Saving energy is nothing new for German home owners — simply because oil, gas, electricity and coal have always been considerably more expensive in Germany than in America. In the summer time, there will be no heating except during extremely cold spells. Air conditioning is only found in very modern offices, hotels and restaurants. Daylight is used whenever possible — and it is rarely so hot that one has to close curtains and shutters against too much sunshine.

Cherished Privacy

More closed doors

More fences between homes

Newcomers are not greeted on arrival

Living in a German House

Foreign customs can be interesting — even fascinating — from a distance. But when it comes to living in close contact with the inhabitants of another country, where the different customs really clash, ill feelings often arise from seemingly minor misunderstandings.

Renting an Apartment

German laws and customs with regard to apartment leasing differ considerably from those in the United States.

First of all, finding a suitable apartment at a reasonable price is not at all easy. Luxury apartments at high rents are easy to find, but normal, nice, comfortable but reasonably priced apartments or houses, not too far from the city centers, are difficult to get hold of. Therefore, unless you have much money to spend, house hunting will take considerable time, patience, and effort.

Furnished apartments are relatively rare. Unfurnished is usually just that in Germany — no light fixtures, built-ins, closets, kitchen cupboards or appliances — just bare walls. Unless you are lucky and find a place through friends or through a newspaper ad, you will probably need the ser-vices of a rental agent or real estate broker (Wohnungs- or Hausmakler, Immobilien-makler). In dealing with a Makler, keep in mind that normally you don't pay any kind of administrative fees (Bearbeitungsge-bühren) and that you should not pay the commission (Courtage) before actually signing the rental agreement (Mietver-trag). The normal fee for the agent is between one and three months' rent. — You may be asked to pay Mietvorauszah-lung (advance payments on the rent) or a contribution to renovating costs or for taking-over built-ins. If Kaution is demand-ed by the landlord, this means that he wants to have "security" in case of damage to his property. This sum will be refund-able in whole or in part, according to the rental contract. Make notes of the condi-tion of the property on moving in (and get it witnessed by the landlord!).

The Extras

The tenant is responsible for the regular maintenance of the rooms, especially in-terior painting and decorating. Utility ser-vices — electricity, gas, water, heating, garbage pick-up, etc. — are usually charged extra, as may be garage rent, use of the garden, chimney sweep, janitor service, etc. In some places, the tenant may be responsible for sweeping the side-walk and clearing away the snow.

Ask questions about all of the above points before you sign, also about the notice of termination (which is often longer here than in the U.S.). Try and get someone experienced to go through the papers with you.

General Rules

As a general rule, no noisy activities are allowed in German apartment houses be-fore 7 or 8 AM, between 1 and 3 PM and after 10 PM. There are also local restric-tions on lawn mowing, etc.

The size of homes is determined by the number of rooms: if you want three bed-rooms, living room, dining room — look for a "5 Zimmer" (room) home. Bathroom, toilet, kitchen and hall areas are not in-cluded in the room count. 2 1/2 rooms does not mean bedroom, living room plus shower/bath (American style), but two rooms plus a small size room.

Problems with Electrical Appliances

Electricity in Germany is 220 Volt — 50 cycle (in USA 110 Volt — 60 cycle). Small appliances can be easily used with a trans-former (Transformator), however it is better not to use appliances with heating coils (toaster, iron, hair dryer) as after a while the coils may burn out! Lamps can be converted by changing the plug and using German light bulbs. Not suitable for use are American TV sets, record players, tape recorders, electric clocks.

The majority of German homes do not have a central hot water system, therefore German washers and dishwashers have built-in water heaters. An American washer or dryer will work with a transformer built in it.

Nearly all German wall sockets are of the round prong type, and only the "Schuko" plug, fitted with a special grounding wire, will fit into it. Electrical shops should have adapter plugs (Zwischenstecker) to convert flat prongs to round.

Different Sizes and Devices

Curtains and draperies are expensive (as are all materials); also the curtain rod system is different. If you bring curtains, bring the rods, hooks and installation devices, too. German lampshades will not fit American or English lamps.

Bed Linen

Bed linen here is quite different from what you're used to. You start with a bottom sheet on the mattress, but instead of adding further layers (top sheet and blankets), you pack a feather-bed (Federbett) in a special covering which encloses it like an envelope.

Sperrmüll

If you wonder about the piles of bulky trash items that decorate the streets of your area every few months, often thoroughly searched by bargain hunters before being hauled away by the garbage men with their big trucks — this is "Sperrmüll," the regular day on which you can get rid of all the large junk that won't fit in your garbage can. Simply put it out onto the curb on the eve of "Sperrmülltag" (ask your landlord or the neighbors for the exact dates and times).

On other days, usually monthly, the Red Cross and other welfare organizations collect bundled newspapers and magazines and old clothes.

Radio and TV

Getting a Phone

The German TV and Radio system works completely different from the American system. It is neither commercial nor government-controlled, but supervised by civic boards made up of representatives of the political parties, trade unions, churches, education, youth organizations, etc. Efforts to start commercial programs are under way, however. So far, there are only two national networks and one "third program" in each region.

Although there is some advertising on German TV, generally packed into several short broadcasts at the beginning of the evening programs, the main source of income is the operating fee which each radio and television owner pays to the "G.E.Z." (Gebühreneinzugszentrale der Rundfunkanstalten). Registration forms (Rundfunk-Anmeldung) are available at all banks and Sparkassen.

Only three channels to choose from, but uninterrupted by commercials.

When renting a house or apartment, see whether there is a telephone already installed which you can take over from the previous tenant. You fill in a form which you get at the post office and which is called "Antrag auf Übertragung eines Fernsprechanschlusses." This you send to the respective "Anmeldestelle für Fernmeldeeinrichtungen." (In Germany, all telecommunications are operated by the post office.) The form for applying for a new installation is called "Antrag auf Einrichtung eines Fernsprechanschlusses."

Once your telephone is installed and connected, you become a subscriber and are obliged to pay your monthly phone bill (Fernmelderechnung). It may be higher than you expect, as telephoning is considerably more expensive in Germany than in the U.S., particularly long-distance. More about using the phone in Germany on pages 81—83.

A practical tip: take a look at the "Buchstabiertafel — Inland" on one of the first pages of your telephone directory. Try to learn the German pronunciation of those words — you may need them when spelling your name or other foreign names to Germans who do not know English!

Your Account With a German Bank

The German banking scene is dominated by three large commercial banks (Deutsche Bank, Dresdner Bank, and Commerzbank) with branch offices all across West Germany; in addition, there are very sizable regional banks and hundreds of savings banks (Sparkassen). The Post Office, too, offers banking services.

To open an account is easy; you merely have to offer identification. There are current accounts (Girokonto) and interest-bearing accounts (Sparkonto).

If your initial deposit is an American check, it may take up to three weeks to be credited to your account. Cashing foreign-currency checks or remitting foreign currency is expensive.

Perhaps the most surprising feature to an American is the use of so-called "transfer orders" (Überweisungen), by which you direct your bank to transfer a particular sum from your account to the account of someone else, even if it is with another bank in another city; this will be accomplished within one or two days. In other words, you do not write checks and mail them individually to your suppliers, but rather prepare transfer orders on your bank's specially-provided forms and deliver them or mail them to your bank. The next day they will deduct the sum from your account and, through the banks' clearing system, eventually the credit will appear on your supplier's bank statement, together with a copy of the transfer order you wrote.

Standing orders (Dauerauftrag) and automatic collections from your account for regular but varying payments (Abbuchung) are also very common services of German banks.

Bank statements (Kontoauszüge) will be sent to you (at cost) or can be picked up monthly at the bank by yourself.

Checks (Schecks) are also available, of course. If you mail a check, be sure to mark it with two lines across the left upper corner, adding the words "nur zur Verrechnung" (for deposit only). The check will not be returned to you after cashing but your bank statement will show you when the amount has been deducted.

A special feature are the "eurocheques" which you can ask for generally after having properly conducted your checking account for several months. Your "eurocheque," accompanied by the presentation of the check card, is guaranteed by your bank for up to DM 300,- in 39 European countries, so you can use it to obtain cash from banks as well as to pay bills in shops, hotels and restaurants.

"Zwei Hunderter und vier Fünfziger, bitte!"
(Twoo 100 DM and four 50 DM bills, please!)

The Red Tape: Residence Permit, Work Permit, Registration

Any private person setting up a new residence in Germany, no matter whether he or she is a German citizen or a foreigner, is required by German law to register (anmelden) immediately — within three to seven days — with the local registration office (Einwohnermeldeamt or Polizeirevier). For this purpose, a form called "Anmeldung" (you can get it in stationery shops or the registration office itself) must be filled out, and an adult member of the family or an authorized agent (with a written power of attorney) must submit the form together with the passports of all members of the family.

For any stay exceeding three months, foreigners need a German residence permit (Aufenthaltserlaubnis). This and the work permit (Arbeitserlaubnis), which is limited to your specific job, in case you wish to take up paid employment in Germany, you should obtain before leaving for Germany. You apply for these permits at the German diplomatic or consular representation in the area where you live. You may also need a certificate of employment from your home employer (if you are staying on that company's payroll while working in Germany), your national or an international driver's license, and documents for car transfer.

If you have not yet obtained a residence permit before leaving your home country, you must — after being registered — submit an application (Antrag auf Erteilung einer Aufenthaltserlaubnis) with the local aliens department (Ausländeramt, or whatever the respective local authority may be called). Take your passport, two photos, and a copy of your "Einwohnermeldebestätigung." You will also be required, shortly after application, to take a medical examination at the public health department. Have cash with you when you go there because fees are charged both for the health examination and the Aufenthaltserlaubnis.

The work permit is issued by the employment office (Arbeitsamt) of the German community where you live. You need a residence permit which does not automatically exclude application for a work permit, your passport, and a form filled out by your future employers stating that they wish to employ you. — In general, work permits are available to non-Germans only if a German or other EEC-citizen cannot fill the job. — A special work permit is issued to foreigners married to Germans.

"What, No PTA?" — School Life Is Different

Living in a German town you will soon notice that contrary to the US the school does not play any particular role in the social life of the community.

It's a totally different tradition. In Germany, almost all schools are public, set up and financed by the state, and the teachers are civil servants, hired and paid by the state school authorities. There are no local school boards and no PTA's (although teachers and parents do meet regularly at "Elternabend"). People are thus much less directly involved with school matters than in the States. Another result: the standard of teaching and exams is relatively equal throughout the country. Curricula, however, differ to a great extent.

In the first four grades, all children are together in the "Grundschule" (elementary school); then, with a two-year transition period and depending on their abilities, they may attend either the "Hauptschule" (main school, up to grade 9), "Realschule" (intermediate school, up to grade 10), "Gymnasium" (academically-oriented high school, up to grade 13), or a combination of them all, "Gesamtschule" (comprehensive school).

German schools are "all business," strictly for learning, and not much goes on in the way of social events. They do have regular

German children spend fewer hours at school than American ones, generally staying only until noon or 1 or 2 PM. Hot lunch is not served at school, but at recess they can eat a sandwich brought from home. In the afternoon, German schoolchildren must sit down to a sizable amount of homework.

excursion days (Wandertag) and take annual class trips (Klassenreise).

Only graduates of a Gymnasium (or holders of an equivalent degree) can attend a university, where the emphasis is placed upon specialization (not on a general "liberal arts" education) in an academic or highly technical field, with a first degree roughly equivalent to an American M. A. Many of the fields taught in American colleges (e.g. nursing) are not to be found at the university but rather at technically-oriented schools of higher education with lower entrance requirements (e. g. Realschule graduation). Many teenagers learn an occupation in an apprenticeship combined with vocational school.

More than Americans, German students tend to separate their private lives from school matters. Thus, the American student in Germany will look in vain for commencement ceremonies, school rings, yearbooks, honor societies, or university football clubs. The traditional fraternities still do exist at German universities but political student associations dominate the scene today. — All in all: a relatively high general standard of education, but less fun at school.

Going to Church?

"Religion: It scarcely plays any role today in the land where the Reformation was born. American religion has simple messages to present to churches that are often packed. German churches are scholarly, liberal — and empty." This is how an American journalist described the situation of the churches in Germany. A harsh judgment, and quite true.

Almost 90 % of the West German population belong to either the Roman Catholic or the Evangelical-Lutheran Church (about half and half), but the majority do not participate actively in church affairs.

On the whole, relations between churches and their members are much less close and personalized here than in the States. Except perhaps for small Catholic congregations, it means little for a person's social standing whether he is an active church-goer or not. Also, through treaties with the German government, the big churches have a guaranteed annual income from their members: if a taxpayer lists his religious affiliation, a church tax is collected by the revenue office and given to the church of his choice.

As a result of historical developments, Northern Germany is primarily Protestant, while the South and West of the country are primarily Catholic. The pattern is gradually changing, however, on account of the population's increasing mobility.

In German Restaurants and Hotels

Eating Out

In restaurants, it's "Gentlemen First!"

Choosing a Place to Eat

The time will come in Germany when you just have to find a place to eat without the help of a German friend or a restaurant guide.

"Fast food" is not as frequently found in Germany as it is in the States, although chances are that in or near any railway station you will hit upon a "Schnellimbiss" (snack bar) or a "Pizzeria."

But perhaps you would prefer going to a German restaurant offering a full range of meals. How do you avoid the fancy places with astronomical prices? Just look for the menu posted at the street front — it will show you the price range and choice of food available.

Men Enter Restaurants First

Many Americans wonder whatever happened to "ladies first" when they see that in Germany men precede women in entering a restaurant. This exception from the rule is clearly a remainder from times when the man was the one to decide whether the locality was fit for the woman to enter. In entering first, he could also screen her from curious stares and relieve her of the task of choosing a table.

No Hostess to Seat You

Contrary to American custom, there are no hostesses in German restaurants to greet and seat you. Normally, you look for a free table yourself. In restaurants of the higher price range, a waiter will approach you and suggest a table or lead you to the table that has been reserved for you.

Calling the Waiter

Asking for the menu, just say "die (Speise-) Karte, bitte!" Never ask for "das Menü" in this case, as that would mean ordering a complete meal! The waiter (der Kellner) is addressed as "Herr Ober" (no matter whether he is the headwaiter — Oberkellner — or not), the waitress as "Fräulein." In small towns and villages, the local Gasthaus or inn is often a family enterprise, where the proprietor and his wife wait on their guests themselves. In such a place, you would call the proprietor "Herr Wirt" and his wife "Frau Wirtin."

Service is slow in many German restaurants. Not only do you have to wait a long time for your meal but often it takes considerable time to get hold of the waiter when you want to pay. If you call him and he replies "sofort" (right away), don't take it literally — it may take him another ten minutes. There is quite a labor shortage in the hotel and catering trade.

Ordering Dinner

Ordering a dinner à la carte is difficult for a foreigner, though fortunately most waiters in German restaurants know a little English. It's simplest to order a "Gedeck" or "Menü" which is a complete dinner with soup (die Suppe) and dessert (der Nachtisch). For à la carte-ordering, see our vocabulary on page 137. Bread or rolls are rarely served with hot meals in Germany. If you order them, there will be a small charge, and also for butter which must be ordered.

Paying the Check

How does one ask for the check? "Herr Ober, ich möchte zahlen!" or "meine Rechnung, bitte!" or very short, "Zahlen, bitte!" Normally, you pay the waiter at your table, rarely at the counter or cash register.

"Herr Ober!"

Tipping

10 to 15 per cent for service (Bedienung) and 13 per cent for value-added tax (Mehrwertsteuer) is included in the prices.

Although an extra tip is not necessary, most people do round the bill off to the nearest Mark or more, according to the amount to be paid and the service rendered. For instance, if the check amounts to DM 11,35 you may say "Zwölf Mark, bitte!" to the waiter, thus indicating that you expect change only for twelve marks and that the rest is for him. Usually the tip is thus given directly to the waiter upon paying and is not left on the table when leaving the place. But to repeat: you are under no obligation to tip, especially not if the service has been poor.

Checks, Credit Cards

It is still rather unusual in German restaurants to pay with a check or a credit card, although attempts are being made to popularize these methods of payment over here, too.

Something on Drinking Habits

No Ice Water?

"Eine Maß"

The Wine Ritual

What They Drink

Germans, it is true, drink a lot of beer — in Bavaria, 230 liters annually per head of the population — but they drink even more coffee. Milk follows in the third place, then come mineral water and "Limonaden" (carbonated soft drinks), tea, wine, and fruit juices.

No Ice Water

Perhaps because the climate is cool enough, the custom of automatically serving ice water in restaurants is not known. Hardly ever will you see a German drink plain water with meals, mostly beer or wine instead. Waiters will look at you strangely and claim it's unhealthy if you order tap water (Leitungswasser) — but they will bring it if you insist, probably thinking secretly that you want to down a pill! Of course, you may drink mineral water (Mineralwasser), fruit, or a soft drink — or nothing at all. Nobody drinks coffee with warm meals in Germany, though, although sometimes immediately afterwards.

Germans like their beer cool, but not ice-cold. It is served either by the bottle (Flasche) or on draft (vom Faß). You order, for instance: "ein kleines Bier" or "ein kleines Helles" or "ein kleines Pils," "einen Halben" or "eine halbe Maß" (half liter), "eine Maß" (one liter), "ein Alt" (dark), "ein Bock" (strong). Average places will usually have only a local or nationally known brand; fancier establishments will serve several well-known brands. "Ein Schoppen" means a quarter of a liter (approximately half a pint) of open wine. 1/2 Fl. means a half bottle.

The Wine Ritual

When wine is served in Germany, the waiter will first show the bottle label to the person who ordered it and will then pour a small amount into his glass. The guest samples the wine — with a connoisseur's air — and then decides whether it is all right and neither too cold nor too warm. That a guest rejects the wine happens very rarely, by the way; usually, he will just nod his approval.

"To Your Health!"

Before the first sip of beer or wine, raise your glass toward your companion and say "Zum Wohl" or "Prost" — both mean "to your health."

The Old Inns

Why is it that so many hotels and inns in German towns have the same names?

In the early Middle Ages lodging for travelers was mostly in the cloisters. The inns and hotels which later sprang up in the neighborhood of these cloisters took names coming from the Old and New Testament. Thus we find hotels called "Engel" (Angel), "Löwe" (Lion), "Stier" (Bull) and "Adler" (Eagle) — the symbols of the Evangelists —, "Drei Mohren" and "Drei Könige" (Three Moors and Three Kings) — the three kings are the symbol of traveling —, "Rose" and "Lilie" (Rose and Lily) — these two flowers represent the Virgin Mary — and the "Lamm" (Lamb), the Lamb of God.

Germany's postal system (begun in 1450) also played a role in the naming of the old inns and restaurants. Many of the establishments which sprang up around the postal stations received names such as "Goldenes Posthorn," "Alte Post," and "Neue Post" or "Zur Post." "Zum" or "Zur" means "to the sign of."

From Ratskeller to Snack Bar

The variety of eating and drinking places in Germany is enormous. In the smaller towns the best places to eat are usually the hotels. **Gasthöfe, Gasthäuser, Gaststuben** and **Gastwirtschaften** are (or include) restaurants.

The more pretentious German restaurants have gone through an astonishing development in the last ten years. With growing prosperity and availability of first-class ingredients, a rather sophisticated gourmet cuisine has come into being. Some top German restaurants come close to the best in French cooking now, and of course their prices are top-notch to match.

Weinstuben (wine parlors) often do not serve complete lunches and dinners, but they can provide you with substantial snacks with your wine.

Bräus (restaurants often featuring a special brand of beer) and **Bierkeller** (beer cellars) usually have plenty of food on hand as well as beer.

Cafés (not to be mistaken for American coffee-houses) sometimes offer hot dishes, too. At any rate, they can produce enough incidental food to satisfy any reasonable person. **Konditoreien** are pastry shops.

A **Ratskeller** is the basement of the city hall (Rathaus). The city fathers once repaired to a Ratskeller table to tip a few and take a meal. Many a Ratskeller has disappeared. Wherever a small-town Ratskeller survives, the beer and fillet steaks are likely to be better than anywhere else in town.

Moreover, there is now a large variety of foreign restaurants — Chinese, Greek, Italian places, steak houses, pizzerias, and what have you.

A **Selbstbedienungs-Restaurant** is similar to the American self-service cafeteria.

Lokal and **Kneipe** are colloquial words for pubs or bars.

A **Schnellimbiss, Schnellgaststätte** or **Imbisstube** is a snack bar. At a Schnellimbiss you will be able to get a couple of sausages with bread and mustard (Würstchen mit Brot und Senf) and a soft drink or beer for a reasonable price. You usually eat standing at a counter or a small round table.

The Bratwurst is fat, white and spicy, the Currywurst is similar but served with a curry catsup; Bockwurst is longer and red, something like a thicker American hot dog. The Frankfurter is thinner and usually sold in pairs. — At an Imbiss sausages are eaten using the fingers, often with the help of a small cardboard slip. You don't get a bun, though often a slice of bread or a small roll is served with your sausage.

Sandwiches are usually open-face, with no bread on top (an exception are those on a roll). Most common are Schinkenbrot (ham on bread) and Käsebrot (cheese on bread).

Other fast-food places also sell pizza and US-style hamburgers and hot dogs as well as the universal grilled chicken (Brat-hähnchen).

Mahlzeit!

Sometimes you hear Germans greet each other with "Mahlzeit" at lunchtime. "Ge-segnete Mahlzeit" means literally "may your meal be blessed" but the more general meaning is "I hope you will enjoy (or have enjoyed) your meal."

More Peculiarities About the Gasthaus

"Regular Table"

In very many German "Gasthäuser" and less pretentious hotels you will find one special table reserved for the local cronies who regularly come together there, usually toward evening, to have a beer, argue politics and perhaps play skat (a card game). This table, usually with its bare wooden top polished from daily use, frequently bears the sign "Stammtisch" (regular table) or a little banner. So when looking for a table, don't be surprised if the management suggests you choose a table other than this one.

Sharing Tables

Except for high-priced restaurants, the practice of sharing tables if there is no free table left is quite common, particularly in southern Germany. Of course, one must ask permission of those seated at the table before seating oneself: "Entschuldigen Sie, ist hier noch frei?" The answer is mostly, "Ja, bitte sehr!" Just before starting to eat, those sharing a table often wish each other "Guten Appetit!" The answer is "Danke." "Gleichfalls" means "the same to you."

A "Stammtisch" for the local regulars.

"Entschuldigen Sie, bitte, ist hier noch frei?"
— "Ja, bitte sehr!"

Meal Times

In most German restaurants, hot food (warme Speisen) is to be had only during the lunch and dinner hours (snack bars, of course, are an exception). You may be able to get hot food at night, but don't count on it. Hot food in the afternoon is even more difficult to get.

Closing Times

How late at night will you be able to get a beer in a German Gaststätte?

Closing hours for drinking places are normally set by the communities, but there are many exceptions. 1 a.m. is the general limit on weekdays, but that does not mean that places cannot close earlier — many do. On Saturday nights, the closing hours are often extended to 2 a.m. Sunday morning. It is also common to grant waivers in night-life districts. Berlin has no officially-fixed closing hours at all.

"Restrooms"

Europeans are often amused when they learn about American efforts to avoid using the word "toilet." In the U.S., words like powder room, rest room, etc. can present considerable problems to female visitors from the Continent. Over here, people have always been less prudish and more direct in such matters. In a German restaurant, for instance, it is absolutely normal, if you want to go to the bathroom, to ask a waiter "Wo ist die Toilette, bitte?"

Usually, there will be a sign pointing to "Toiletten" (plural) or "W.C." (meaning water closet). "Damen" of course means ladies, "Herren" men. Sometimes, signs just say "sie" (she) and "er" (he), or male and female figures are used as symbols.

In contrast to most other public buildings (where the fee is usually 30 Pfennige) restaurants are not allowed to charge a fee for using the "Toilette." They may, however, charge you for using the washbasin, soap and towel. If there is an attendant, a tip is expected.

Public toilets at Autobahn "Raststätten" (restaurant-plus-gas station complexes) are often terrible, by the way. Try to avoid them if you can!

Two Valuable Guides — VARTA and MICHELIN

There surely are many good hotels and restaurants in Germany, but where exactly are they to be found? Where can you expect first-class food at a reasonable price? Where do you sleep undisturbed by traffic noise? Where are the main sights of the town? Where are hotels in castles?

All these questions and many, many more are answered in the "VARTA-Führer durch Deutschland" (VARTA Guide through Germany) and the red "MICHELIN Deutschland" guide. The newest editions of these guides are published every spring.

Symbol Language

Although they are in German, the books also can be highly recommended to English-speaking readers, as the signs used throughout these guides not only are very clear but also are fully explained in English. The foreword, the table of contents and the notes for users also are given in English.

Both guides list hotels and restaurants in thousands of German towns. For the hotels, they give five or six different standards and all additional information available and necessary. Restaurants are classified according to their rates (three classes in VARTA, five in MICHELIN).

Both guides are real goldmines of practical information for the tourist in Germany. Of course, there are certain differences between them: we feel, for instance, that VARTA uses clearer, simpler symbols which make it easier to find everything at a glance. VARTA also attaches greater weight to the various standards of the cuisine, being more generous in granting special distinctions to German restaurants than MICHELIN.

Besides the red MICHELIN hotel and restaurant guide there is also a green MICHELIN for Germany, which is a travel guide (and it appears also in English).

What makes these guides especially commendable is the fact that they are completely independent of advertising. All hotels and restaurants are examined by traveling inspectors who remain incognito.

At a German Hotel

"Würden Sie sich bitte eintragen?" (Please fill in the registration form)

If you stay in a moderately priced hotel, you should bring your soap with you!

In some hotels, particularly those of the upper price-range, shoes still shed their dirt overnight. Leave a coin tip in them.

At a German Hotel

How to Find a Room

The safest way is, of course, to reserve a room in advance, either through a travel agency or, if you know a hotel, by calling, or by dropping a line yourself (English will do), with a self-addressed stamped card inside.

If you arrive without a room, in many German towns you can make use of the services of a room referral agency, called "Zimmernachweis," which often is in or near the railway station. It charges a small fee for locating a room in the price range you indicate. You can also just try the hotels that come along your way. In addition to hotels, look for signs that say "Pension." Pensionen are generally cheaper and plainer than hotels, and usually have no rooms with bath. "Fremdenzimmer" or "Zimmer frei" means rooms in private homes. Motels are extremely rare in Germany. In big cities, taking a chance in looking for a hotel room can be risky, as often there are conventions or fairs going on that occupy all available hotel rooms.

The most reasonable overnight lodgings are the youth hostels ("Jugendherbergen"). They are clean and generally easily accessible. Each individual who wants to stay in a youth hostel must have a membership card. You would do well to get one before leaving the States, as the charge is fairly high in Germany. The disadvantage is that they do not allow you to come home later than 10 p. m.

There are more single rooms (Einzelzimmer) available here than in most U.S. hotels. They are relatively more expensive than two-bed rooms (Doppelzimmer).

Bath Must Be Ordered

If you wish to have a room with private bath and toilet ("mit Dusche (shower)/Bad (bath) und W. C. (water closet)"), both must be specifically ordered but are not always available. If not, there is usually at least one bathroom with shower on each floor at the disposal of all hotel guests (Etagenbad). However, you should always announce your intention to use the public bath before actually doing so, as a fee will be charged for it. Heating, too, may cost extra in hotel rooms. Americans sometimes resent all these extra charges for small extra services in European hotels, but Europeans, as a rule, prefer to know precisely what they're paying for instead of having all the little extras wrapped up in a single amount.

Room and Board

In resort towns, if you stay at least three days, many places offer inclusive rates for accommodation and meals (Halbpension or Vollpension).

Registration Forms

Most Americans traveling in Europe for the first time are a bit irked by the necessity to fill out official forms when registering in a hotel (home address, date of birth, nationality, etc.). These forms must be filled out by all guests, German or foreign. They are required by law, in the interest of public safety. If you intend to stay in a moderately priced German hotel, bring your soap and wash cloths along. All hotels supply towels, but only the more expensive ones supply soap.

German hotels of the upper price-range still offer a service that may make up for the absence of shoe-shine boys in the streets: if you put your shoes outside your door

46

before you go to bed, a hotel attendant will polish them in the early morning hours. Leave a coin tip in them!

Continental Breakfast

A "continental breakfast" is usually included in the price of the hotel room. Normally it consists of "Kaffee" or "Tee" (you have a choice), "Brötchen" (white rolls), "Schwarzbrot" (brown bread), "Marmelade" (jam) and sometimes "Honig" (honey) and, on request, a soft-boiled egg ("weich gekochtes Ei") served in a little egg cup. If this is not enough you may, of course, order something else, for instance: fried eggs ("Spiegeleier") or scrambled eggs ("Rühreier"). Germans often also ask for "Aufschnitt" (assorted cold cuts and cheese) for breakfast.

If you go out, it is customary in German hotels to leave the key (Schlüssel) with the reception desk and ask for it again when coming back (just say your room number, followed by "Bitte").

Paying and Tipping

In all German hotels, pensions, etc., you pay when you check out. A service charge will be included in the bill, therefore you are not expected to tip anybody — except for the boy who carried your bag to your room (not under a mark) and the reception clerk, if he has helped you with some special service.

The Portier Helps You

The reception clerk, or in German, the Portier, is the man to turn to for almost everything. He speaks English, he will mail your letters, he will take phone calls when you are out. He tells you which train, bus, boat, or plane to take. He will get you tickets for them, as well as for theaters, etc. He will recommend the best nightspots, the stores in which to buy souvenirs. He will exchange your money after hours. He will also make reservations for you in the next town as he knows all the Portiers there. Even in desperate situations a good Portier can almost always find a way — if he is tipped according to the difficulty of the task. . .

More About German Food

That all Germans eat sauerkraut and love heavy meals is a standard part of the German image abroad. It's a myth like the lederhosen image, and myths die hard. Actually, if you go to a German restaurant and ask for sauerkraut, you may even get it!

Myth or not, the reality is that a quiet but very remarkable revolution has taken place in German eating habits during the last decades. With growing prosperity and more money in their hands than ever before, Germans have discovered the good life — travel, elegant clothing, well-furnished homes, comfortable cars, and last but not least the delights of good eating and drinking. Of all food products, wine and cheese have had the highest growth rate in Germany (almost 50%) in the last decade. The following figures also illustrate the change:

Annual consumption per inhabitant/kg

	25 years ago	now
fresh fruit	47	98
meat	34	87
eggs	8	17
potatoes	186	83
bread	80	63

The German housewife is deluged with ever new, ever more enticing and colorful cookbooks. There's a boom in restaurant guides, and no popular magazine can do without a regular recipe column, often presenting exotic or even haute-cuisine gourmet recommendations.

But the good old German standard fare is still there, too, and you will find it on the menus from the Danish border down to the Bavarian Alps. The following pages invite you to "Gourmet's Germany."

A Short Guide to Gourmet's Germany

The gourmet's map of Germany is dotted with excellent restaurants and lovely pubs, with noteworthy dishes, great wines, wonderful beer. Regional and individual diversity mark the culinary and gustatory offerings of the country; they must be sought for, and sampled, in the manner of those Germans who take their eating and drinking seriously, as many do indeed. To join them in this noble pursuit does not merely satisfy your palate; one way to the heart of a foreign country — and surely not the worst — leads through the stomach.

Not all the food that awaits you in Germany is German food. Sometimes it has merely a dash, an overtone, a soupçon to remind you of its German provenience.

In good and very good German restaurants, you will find all the international standard dishes, that is, the steaks, chops, chickens that are served and deservedly popular elsewhere, too.

Next to these standbys, you will also find on many German menus a surprising number of more or less exotic dishes; imported from abroad, they have become part and parcel of German routine fare. Next to typically German and truly international dishes, you will be offered, say, shark's fin soup, curry dishes transplanted from Asia to Germany, goulash (and goulash soup which Germans like to eat as a pick-me-up all by itself, late at night after a show, say) and shashlik which has gained great German popularity since the end of the war; this Eastern European dish, invented by shepherds of the steppe broiling their lamb and vegetables on a long spit over the open fire, is served now in luxury restaurants as well as at primitive street corner stands.

If only for a change between your German explorations, you can also explore other countries from your German dinner table, and eat your way around the world without leaving the country. Germany, a cosmopolitan country nowadays, is studded with foreign restaurants — authentic and good Italian places, as well as Swedish, French, Hungarian, Yugoslav, Russian, Greek cookeries. Also, a great number of Chinese restaurants have spread all over Germany.

But it is German cooking that awaits your discovery. Let's assume your guide and dinner companion is a German gourmet who, like every "Feinschmecker," has certain preferences and dislikes of a highly personal nature and with all his expertness remains a searcher for new and fine food. What will he order on the festive occasion?

One thing to remember is that good eating, when taken as seriously as it deserves to be and as it is taken in good German places, requires time — from the cook, the waiter and particularly from you, yourself. Don't get impatient if at least an hour, and probably more, is consumed by your lunch and your dinner; in return, it will be a more well-rounded — and healthier! — experience than a meal gulped down in a jiffy.

Appetizers

The curtain rises with the "Vorspeise," the appetizer. In contrast to French hors d'oeuvres or Scandinavian smorgasbrod with their collection of different appetizers composed according to custom or to the cook's tastes, only one single item is chosen individually from the menu.

The offerings will get more appetizing as you travel northwards toward the ocean, reaching a crescendo in Hamburg and other seaside places; fish — smoked, pickled, or in aspic jelly — is the most important mainstay of "Vorspeisen." You may pick herring — rollmops, matjes fillet, Bismarck herring — or climb a step higher on the gourmet's scale and try salmon. Another German appetizer sometimes frightens Americans before they have experienced its delights: It is eel, that highlight of German appetizer trays. Rather than shrimps, you will find salty, delicious crayfish and fresh crabmeat to ring in your meal. Only most elegant places serve lobster, a luxurious and, therefore, expensive dish in Germany.

Moving away from the coast you will still find all these seafood delights plus an increasing variety of cold cuts, "wurst," and hams eaten as appetizers. Almost every town, and certainly every region, has one or more sausage specialties of its own. Other such specialties extend all the way from the noble Pomeranian smoked breast of goose ("geräucherte Gänsebrust") to the earthy Franconian pressack liver cheese ("Leberkäse"), the salad of beef mouth ("Ochsenmaulsalat") and the rustic Bavarian sausage of 68 varieties.

On less festive occasions, each of these "Vorspeisen" may serve as a whole meal, or sometimes an in-between meal — the second breakfast, say, which Munich burghers take between breakfast and lunch, or the twilight snack before dinner. At a gala meal, a soup follows the appetizer, and this is followed in turn by the main dish or dishes — fish and/or meat.

Fish and Meat

As to fish, there is again much local variation. In the South, it may come from a neighboring brook or stream or lake. Some types of fish are peculiar only to one stream or lake. Examples are the "Renken" of the Upper Bavarian mountain lakes, the "Felchen" of Lake Constance and the speckled brook trout from Alpine streams, all collector's items of fish at its best. Trout ("Forelle"), though, is also served further North, where the rivers yield other exciting contributions to the menu — eel, pike, tench, sole, turbot (Aal, Hecht, Schleie, Seezunge, Steinbutt). And then there is carp (Karpfen) which, deservedly, ranks as high on the German palate scale as steaks and lobsters on the American. Carefully cultivated in special carp lakes for decades, and cooked in several different ways, it can be the highlight of any gala dinner.

At the next course you will discover that "Sauerbraten" in Germany does not even resemble the dish of the same name which sometimes in America is supposed to represent "German cooking." It can be a work of art, and the same goes for the other tired standby of "German" cooking in America, the "Schnitzel." Although often it may be just a soggy cutlet shamefully camouflaged under a crust of crumbs, in good restaurants German "Schnitzels" comprise a whole family of tastily arranged veal cutlets in cream sauce ("Rahmschnitzel"), or cooked in paprika ("Paprikaschnitzel"), or garnished with mushrooms ("Jägerschnitzel"). The "Wiener Schnitzel," of course, comes first on the explorer's list, but he must also sample the "Schnitzel à la Holstein," the king of all Schnitzels, invented by and named after a hard-working old bachelor diplomat who liked all the best on one plate. Framed by tiny portions of smoked salmon, caviar and other rare hors d'oeuvres stimulating the taste buds at the same time that the Schnitzel satisfies them, it is a highly unorthodox yet exciting culinary creation.

In the eyes of many foreign, particularly American, students of this subject as well as of your guide, venison is probably the most distinctive, if not unique feature of the haute cuisine Allemande. In all first-rate and most good restaurants, you will find at least one venison dish; yet if you happen to be in a village and see a hunter returning with his bag, you had better stay for a day — chances are you will be able to eat it on the very next day and love it. In addition to deer, you may also be lucky enough to be regaled with fallow deer or buck, perhaps even with wild boar and chamois in the Bavarian mountains.

Also still deservedly appreciated in German eating are the — often splendidly cooked, fried, sautéed — inner parts of animals, particularly liver (try Berliner Leber, flavored with onions and slices of apples), brains, heart, spleen, kidneys and sweetbreads. Another specialité de la maison in Germany widely unknown in America and therefore first shocking, then intriguing, finally delighting American culinary explorers is the Tartar Beefsteak — superior beef finely minced and served with a raw egg, paprika, pepper, capers, minced onions, sometimes additional spices on the side. You prepare it yourself — first stirring the egg into the meat which

gives it consistency, then adding all the other paraphernalia, before you spread it onto your heavily buttered rye bread.

Desserts

If cheese, pastry, pies, cakes or ice cream top the dinner, the choice is up to you — and the choice will be as hard as can be. Some German cheese — particularly the camembert laced with champignons, and the Tilsiter — are considered by cheese experts among the best, and as far as sweet bakery is concerned, Germans are undoubtedly past masters.

The Regional Specialties

When you have eaten your way through a number of these fine standard dishes of a fine standard dinner, you really have only begun the most delicious phases of your explorer's trip into the interior of good German life. Here and there you will discover new gastronomic delights, mostly the speciality of one region, or town, if not restaurant. You will come upon Munich's white sausages ("Weißwürste") made from an inimitable mixture of veal and pork, and

preferably eaten between midnight and noon; or Nuremberg's famous "Bratwürste," pork sausages as small as a baby's finger, highly spiced, served by the half dozen with sauerkraut on a pewter plate; or Hamburg's "Aal Suppe," eel soup, which is the German answer to the bouillabaisse; or that exciting culmination of a well-heeled German farmer's holiday table, the roast goose, which can stand competition with the best Thanksgiving turkey.

And now: "Guten Appetit!" — as the Germans say when they sit down to eat.

Kurt St. Baer

How About a Cup of "Kaffee"?

Coffee drinking is highly revered in Germany. The preparation, the drinking and the enjoying of a good cup of coffee is an art.

During a visit with an American family encamped near Mannheim the subject of coffee came up. This young dashing wife and her captain spouse had traveled all through Germany and looked in all of the various interesting nooks and corners, visited the Black Forest, Oberammergau and Hamburg, but had never been inside a Café-Konditorei. Our American wife said that someone in the States had said German coffee is bitter, black and tastes awful, and she had been afraid ever since to take the chance.

"Sometimes I was tempted," she said, "by all those wonderfully decorated cakes, but always I lost my nerve just before going in."

Well, you adventuresome Americans, have no fear. Go into the next coffeehouse you come to and have a really good cup of coffee. Speaking as an American, I met the German cup of coffee head on with my eyes wide open and enjoyed it very much. These coffeehouses over here are also one of the best examples of German "Gemütlichkeit." You can order one cup of that stuff and sit for hours if you want to. Write your letters, read your papers, discuss politics; no one will rush you or even expect you to drink a second cup unless you want to. In these shops you will also find assortments of cakes that you never dreamed of. Fruit cakes, layer cakes, fudge and nougat-filled cakes. The German bakers take much trouble with their cakes.

Let us look at what they go through just for a cup of coffee. When you go into the shop the first thing that usually catches the eye is a large, highly-polished metal machine, with much piping and many spigots and handles. Steam pours out of it, people run round it putting things in and taking things out. And to think all it does is just make coffee. As it is heavily taxed, coffee here is four times as expensive as it is in America, therefore all the best techniques of science and plumbing are put into the production of a cup of coffee. The right amount of that brown powder is put into a little container with a piece of filter paper which in turn is inserted into the machine. Steam, boiling water and pressure force the best of the flavor out of the coffee into your cup. The machine works, the people cheer and the coffee ist brought to you hot, full of aroma and really good.

By this time you have been to the buffet and with trembling finger have already picked out a few pieces of butter creme layer cake with a portion of "Schlagsahne" (whipped cream — don't forget the Schlagsahne, nothing is complete without it). You now sit down and lean back. You breathe in the delectable aroma of the coffee. You add the right amount of sugar and, if you like, cream or condensed milk to suit your taste. Then comes the first sip. Do not attract attention to yourself but breathe in and sigh a little bit. Now you have broken the ice. Slowly and with much ritual you eat your cake and drink your coffee. When you have finished — relax.

Most Europeans still think that none of the pleasures of life should be rushed and that means expecially drinking coffee.

On Wining in Germany

As Americans are used to imbibing before and, perhaps, after eating, so are Germans used to imbibing during their meals. Although there is no law against taking a drink before lunch or dinner, it is rather unusual, whereas beer or wine with a meal are taken for granted. To pick the right wine or, on very festive occasions, the right wines is a ritual, a science, an important decision and a test of savoir-faire not to be taken lightly.

Witness the faces of German diners as they decide on their choice, once the waiter has opened the "Weinkarte" before them. A sudden look of seriousness overcomes the table companions, suspense hovers over them, and they return to relieved gaiety only after they have made their decision, tested it with a first, tiny sip and found it good. Although it may well take a lifetime of study and experience to become "The Complete Winesman," the amateur sipper and lay gourmet can easily master the fundamentals — and they are pleasant enough to learn.

Wines, his teacher would set out to explain, are distinguished by and classified according to their regions of origin. Next come their particular vineyards, and then their vintage years. Sometimes they also are marked by the time in the year's season when their grapes were picked. If they were gathered after the month of the general vintage, which is possible only with grapes of extraordinary quality, the wine is labeled "Spätlese." To indicate an even later moment at which they were taken from the vine, the terms "Auslese, Beeren-auslese, Goldbeerenauslese" and "Trok-kenbeerenauslese" are used. This latter type is the latest, rarest and choicest kind, but all the labels stand for the unusual grade of golden ripeness and sweetness which sets them off from the general vintage; as such, they are sipped after the meal rather than with it.

The names of the regions that distinguish the different kinds of German wine sound like music to the connoisseur. If even the most ignorant layman has heard of Rhine wines, it must be explained that this term really includes three rather different kinds.

First and foremost, there are the wines from the Rhinegau proper, a stretch of land fifteen miles long where the hills framing the Rhine River yield some of the world's most famous and greatest wines — the Johannisberger, the Hochheimer (which, abbreviated to Hock, became the Britsh term for all Rhine wines), the Winkeler and dozens of other brands famed for their rather dry, highly aromatic, smooth and ringing taste.

Next to the Rhinegau grow the Rhinehessen wines, a symphony ranging from light and pleasant notes to fiery accords — from Gau-Bickelsheimer, say, Binger or Oppenheimer, to the world-famous Liebfrauenmilch which grows in a small vineyard yet has given its name to many less distinguished also-rans (since this name is not a protected trade-mark).

The third lovely sister in the Rhinewine family is the Pfälzer, from the Palatinate, again offering a choice from friendly little table wines to the noble, powerful great achievements of winedom. Deidesheim, Forst, Ruppertsberg and Kallstadt are some of the names that go with the wine from the Palatinate.

In the further neighborhood of the Rhine other river valleys supply wines of quite different and often unsurpassed beauty. A favorite is the Moselle, whose wines are extremely fragrant, although in general better in their prime up to five years rather than in old age. Some of the greatest

Moselle wine names are Wehlen, Bernkastel, Ürzig, Zeltingen, Piesport, Domherrenberg, Graach and Trittenheim. The wines from the Saar and the Ruwer resemble those of the Moselle family, while Nahe wines take the middle road between Rhine and Moselle.

Some distance off toward the south grow the wines of Franconia, also called Bocksbeutel from the shape of the low, fat bottle in which they come, or Steinweine, from one particular cluster of vineyards overlooking the town of Würzburg. Pale, fragrant, perfumed with the quintessence of spring flowers, at their best they belong among the world's most prized. They age well. Iphofen, the different Würzburg vineyards (some of the best belonging to and named after hospitals which they keep going) and Randesacker, also Escherndorf, Markt-Einersheim and Homburg, have been identified with great wines of this district.

Most German wines and the truly great among them are white, but there also are splendid red wines; however, they come only from a few vineyards, are produced in small quantities and are not always available. In the expert's opinion, some Spät-burgunder from the Ahr River valley can well stand next to the great Burgundies, as can the Assmannshäuser red wines. In addition, they are supposed to have medicinal qualities, being the only red wines permitted to diabetics. Pfalz and Baden also offer a few pleasant red wines. Baden, to round the picture, produces Germany's only rosé wine, the lovely, lively Schillerwein (to express its faculty to change color — schillern in German — from white to pink red).

Travelers in the winegrowing districts often prefer the vin du pays to more famous wines. It is a deeply satisfying experience to be able to point to a nearby hill, nodding to you through the inn window or winking at you while you sit in the inn garden when the waitress takes your order, and then to get acquainted with the very wine that grew almost before your eyes.

In more elaborate places or in cities, you will have to take potluck, or rather bottle luck, picking from the wine menu a name that attracts you. If you prefer less haphazard methods, you can always tell the waiter what your heart and your palate are after, and he will assist you in your choice.

Slowly, by tempting trial and pleasant error but at any rate happily, will you learn to find your way all by yourself through the vintages and vineyards of Germany. One Munich wine house, Schwarzwälder's, has a wine menu which is a heavy, leatherbound volume of more than one hundred pages; it presents a comprehensive catalogue of truly worthwhile wines of which there are thousands, although hardly more than 150 or 200 attain the upper reaches of greatness. Less ambitious places of high standards — and there is at least one in almost every town! — offer you a choice among several dozen wines which makes things easier for you and is just as much fun.

Kurt St. Baer

German Wine Regions

Here is a chart of Germany's wine-growing districts for your use. It must be taken into consideration that within each area, smaller wine regions exist plus particular vineyards yielding wines having their own special character.

But to explain all of these would require a book. You must, therefore, become acquainted with these wines simply by "tasting," not at all an unpleasant task.

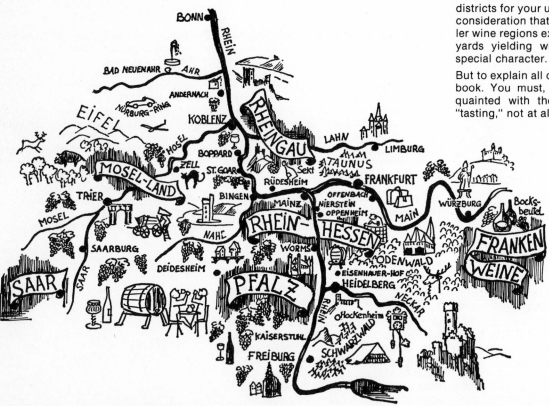

The Individual Regions and Their Wines

Rheingau	Powerful, sweet wines tending to have a fresh taste due to the high percentage of acidity.
Rheinhessen	Fuller and sweeter than those of the Rheingau with rather less character. Home of the famous "Liebfrauenmilch."
Rheinpfalz (Rhine-Palatinate)	Most wines coming from this district are strong but milder ones may be had. Oftentimes have a taste of the soil.
Moselle-Saar-Ruwer	Moselle wines are similar to the Rhine wines, but are lighter and less sweet, the best having an exquisite fragrance and delicacy. Saar and Ruwer wines rank with the Moselles but have their own distinct personality; the ones coming from the Saar being especially fragrant; the Ruwer wines possessing a more spicy, aromatic flavor.
Nahe	The Nahe area produces wines similar to Rhines and Moselles. They are less fruity than the former but fuller than the latter. Excellent general purpose wine, although strong.
Baden	Wines coming from this area are extremely varied; some strong and fiery, others mild.
Ahr	From the valley of the Ahr comes a fiery red wine.
Württemberg	Here again the wines vary, some being strong while others are much milder.
Middle-Rhine (Mittelrhein)	Hearty wines with a touch of the soil.

The Label Tells What's in a Bottle

Deutscher Tafelwein (German Table or Dinner Wine)

This group includes all so-called consumer wines, i.e. the lower price ranges. These wines can be mixed from several wines harvested in different locations of one larger wine-growing area. A name designating a special situation of vineyard ("Lage") is not permitted on the label. However, details like the region, place name, kind of grapes and vintage year may be indicated if they apply to at least 75 per cent of the bottle content. Certain, officially defined improvements of the grape juice are permitted.

Qualitätswein bestimmter Anbaugebiete (Quality Wines from Certain Regions)

These are good wines of the medium price ranges. Quality wine must have been produced in one special wine-growing region. Labels must show an official control number. The kind of grapes used (Riesling, Sylvaner, Müller-Thurgau, Gewürztraminer, Burgunder, etc.) must be indicated. Minor, officially defined improvements of the grape juice are permitted. The prescribed minimum specific gravity of the grape juice lies higher than with table wines. If a special situation of vineyard is indicated, this must apply to at least 75 per cent of the bottle content.

Qualitätswein mit Prädikat (Quality Wines with Distinction)

This is the top group of the quality wines. The wine must come from vineyards of equal situation within one special location, yielding grapes of the same quality and kind. No improvements allowed. Higher minimum specific gravity of the grape juice. Distinctions: Kabinett, Spätlese (late harvested wine), Auslese (selected late harvested wine), Beerenauslese and Trokkenbeerenauslese (raisin wines).

With regard to German champagnes, the following designations are used:

Schaumwein (Sparkling Wine)

The cheapest group, minimum alcohol content 70 grams per liter.

Qualitätsschaumwein or Sekt (Quality Champagne)

Label must show an official control number. Minimum alcohol content 80 grams / liter. Minimum storage time: nine months. This quality may be called "Deutscher Sekt" (German champagne) if at least 60 per cent of the bottle content was made of German-grown grapes.

Deutscher Prädikatssekt (German Quality Champagne With Distinction)

The highest quality, having been produced from at least 75 per cent German grapes and complying with a number of further prescriptions regarding the quality of the grapes used, storage time, etc.

Weinbrand

Finally, with regard to German brandies, they may be called "Weinbrand" only if they have been stored in oak barrels for at least six months and if the label bears an official quality control number.

Top Your Meal With Liquor

According to German custom, you should top your dinner with liquor, although you may well start out with a tumblerful before it begins, too. The surprising variety and richness of German "Schnaps" is little known abroad. German brandy, or "Weinbrand," bears more resemblance in taste to bourbon whisky than to cognacs; German gin — of which Steinhäger is most popular, besides many variations, such as Bommerlunder and Doornkaat — is surely one of the world's best. Germans take their native liquor straight rather than mix it, and it is widely believed that this is a healthy way of drinking. But if you must, you can mix all your familiar vodka and gin drinks by using Steinhäger instead — in fact, Bloody Marys and Screwdrivers made with this German liquor have high quality; and Weinbrand will do in place of whisky when you are out for a Manhattan with German ingredients.

In addition to these two standard drinks of Weinbrand and Steinhäger, Germany offers a plentiful and beautiful choice of hard liquor made from bases other than grapes or grain and equally delicious. The great and good family of German fruit brandies includes Kirschwasser distilled from cherries; Himbeergeist, from raspberries; Erdbeergeist, from strawberries; Pflaumenwasser and Zwetschengeist, from prunes and plums respectively; Wacholder, from juniper berries and Enzian, from gentian, that lovely flower of the Alps. You inhale their distinctive aroma before you sip them. And do not trust them; despite their bucolic basis, they are more powerful than they seem at first.

To drink wine, beer or spirits by themselves after the meal is part of German social life. Wine places — often very old and filled with relics and wine fumes of many centuries — and beer places, sometimes very big, or gigantic like the Munich Hofbräuhaus, the world's hugest pub, also serve the spirits which you may crave. Entertainment is often added — from the zither player discreetly strumming in the corner of the Weinstube to the big and brassy band playing away in the Bräuhaus; but the best entertainment is procured by the drinks themselves and the merrymaking guests and the spirit of the place. You find, of course, also "Bars" most everywhere, but these are considered abodes of high life and night clubs rather than everyday drinking places.

Neither does a German "Café" bear any resemblance to the American establishment of the same name. It is a coffeehouse where you really drink a cup of coffee, perhaps supplemented by a piece of cake or pastry; soft-boiled eggs, or minced meat baked under a thin dough crust, the Pasteten, are usually the main, if not only warm dishes served; but you can also drink wine, beer or liquor here. If the place has a sidewalk café or "Terrasse," all the better; you can enjoy the free entertainment of the passing street scene for a long time. It is also a good place for anyone just to dream and think of many things — including all the fine food and drinks you have enjoyed and will keep enjoying in Germany.

A Good Glass of Beer

If there was a time when mankind was without beer, history has no record of it. It is one of the oldest alcoholic beverages known, and archeologists have found recipes in ancient Egyptian hieroglyphics which prove beer was brewed at least nine thousand years ago.

The recipe has changed little since then. The kind Cleopatra served Anthony must have tasted much like what the Herr Ober serves you today.

Although brewers the world over use approximately the same recipe, the real beer-connoisseur is scandalized at the idea that "beer is beer." Even with two identical recipes, he points out, the end product can be different.

Beer Is Not Beer

The type of water used, for example, is a determining factor. Thus, Munich beer will always taste different from Berlin beer because the water in the two cities tastes different.

Another difference between beers is apparent even to the "beer is beer" drinker. He finds on coming to Germany that beer here often appears rather flat when drunk direct from the refrigerator. This is because in German beers the carbonic acid is produced naturally and never removed from the beer, whereas in the U.S. the carbonic acid is removed and then added artificially just before bottling. In Germany, where the carbonic acid is "bound in," beer will not fizz when it is too cold.

German beer is never at its best at refrigerator temperature. It should be drunk at about 45° F., when it will fizz and be at its optimum flavor.

Another difference between German and American beer is that American beer is always pasteurized. This is not done to kill dangerous bacteria, but to preserve the beer over a longer period. German beer is not pasteurized unless it is to be shipped to other cities or countries. Unpasteurized, it can be kept about two months. Beer drinkers with very developed tastes say pasteurized beer has a slightly breadlike taste, and prefer the unpasteurized variety.

There are many who insist they went to Munich's Oktoberfest and drank beer with 18 % alcohol. They are mistaken. Bock beer, which has the highest alcoholic content, has only 5 % alcohol. When breweries refer to an 18 % beer, they are speaking of the percentage of "wort," not alcohol. What is "wort"? We'll get to that in a little while.

The weakest beer is Malzbier, or malt beer, with less than 1 % alcohol. It is considered very healthy and often given to children and nursing mothers in Germany. The famous Berliner Weissbier also contains only about 1 % alcohol.

Pilsner is the bitterest beer, with the most hops; export beer the most expensive; Märzen has a robustness between Pilsner and Bock and is sold, as its name indicates, in March; Johanniter is another very strong beer, sold the year around.

Breweries Welcome Visitors

Most German breweries welcome visitors and schedule regular tours of the plant. One sees beer in the making, from the unloading of barley to the final bottling. No guests are permitted to leave without sampling the product — not that any try to.

It's no problem locating a brewery. The pungent, almost overpowering smell of malt dominates everything for blocks around. Inside the courtyard of red brick buildings, one sees cheerful employees carrying a half dozen mugfuls of foaming beer to sustain their working colleagues, pony-drawn wagons loaded with beer kegs clattering by, and huge 100-foot-high silos in which the malt is stored.

How It's Made

Only four ingredients are required; a grain (usually barley), hops, yeast and water.

Most barley comes from Southern Germany. After the barley is harvested, it must rest six weeks to absorb oxygen and "store up energy to grow again," as the brewers explain it. Then it is soaked in water and kept in humid air for six days until it sprouts, or germinates, just as seeds do underground in the natural growing process.

This is the beginning of the malting process, and the sprouting barley is referred to as "green malt." It is next put into a kiln and roasted to dry it out, producing "malt," then stored in the huge, 100-feet-high silos.

Brewing is begun when the malt grits is placed in huge copper brewing vats (called mash tuns), mixed with water from the brewery's own wells and boiled. This frees the starch and albumin from the malt husks. The starch is converted into sugar.

This mixture is then transferred to another set of copper vats — the clarification boilers — where the liquid is separated from the husks and solid substances of the malt (spent grains). This is now called "wort."

In a third set of copper vats the "wort" gets literally "hopped-up." Hops are added to give the beer a bitter taste and preserve it. There it is boiled until the desired quantity of water has evaporated.

In the next step, the hops are removed. The spent grains are also saved, to be sold as feed to cattle owners.

Fermentation now begins. This is accomplished by adding yeast. Breweries cultivate their own yeast, and this is the least of their expenses. All that is needed is one yeast cell, which will grow indefinitely and produce all the yeast needed for hundreds of years of operation.

In the fermenting vats, the "wort" expands as the yeast grows, forming great globs of foam. The malt sugar turns into alcohol and carbonic acid, which gives the beer its fizz.

This so-called "green beer" ferments for six to eight days. The yeast settles on the bottom and it, like the hops, is used a second time. Then it is sold to pharmaceutical firms who turn it into a medicine often prescribed to cure pimples.

After fermenting, the beer is stored 12—16 weeks to ripen. Fermentation continues during storage, with excessive carbonic acid escaping through special openings so the container doesn't explode. Then it is poured into kegs or bottled by machines that can fill as many as 15,000 bottles per hour.

Delivery is usually made by modern trucks, but most German breweries use a few dray horses and ponies for sentimental old time's sake.

Like the rest of the brewery employees, the horses are provided a daily beer ration which — in contrast to regulations of most other jobs — must be drunk during working hours. The ponies get a half liter, their human colleagues four times that, but the result is the same — happy, willing workers who don't dread going to work in the morning.

Carlotta Anderson

Beer Is Not Beer

There are so many brands and types of German beer that the foreign visitor is easily confused.

In spite of stiff competition and much concentration in recent years, there are still some 1,500 different breweries in existence, producing approximately 5,000 different brands.

From "Helles" to "Alt"

There are two main groups of beer: the "bottom-brewed" ones are the most popular in Germany, such as "Helles," "Pils," "Export" and "Bock," while the top-brewed beers (fermented according to the older method) include such specialties as the "Altbier" of the Düsseldorf-Münster region, the "Kölsch" of Cologne, the Berlin "Weissbier," and the South-German "Weizenbier."

Over the last decade, Pils beers have become the most popular in Germany, followed by the Export brands. "Alt" seems to be the newest fad.

Canned beer is not very popular here. Only four per cent is bought in throw-away bottles or cans. Ninety per cent of bottled beer is bought by the case, and the bottles are returned.

200 Kinds of Bread — and 1,500 Types of Sausage

The Germans — in spite of all the changes that have taken place in their way of living and way of eating in recent years — are still great bread eaters. They eat bread not only for breakfast but also for supper (called "Abendbrot" — evening bread) and for in-between meals. There are some 200 different kinds of bread in Germany, 30 kinds of rolls (Brötchen, Semmel), and no less than 1,200 different kinds of pastries! Although the North Germans are said to eat even more bread than the South Germans, there is general agreement that it is in the South of the country — the wheat-growing regions — where the art of bread baking really flourishes. The main types of German bread are described below:

Weissbrot and Toastbrot
similar to the standard bread in the U.S., Canada, and Britain — but not the standard bread of the Germans, which is:

Feinbrot or Mischbrot (Graubrot)
made from a mixture of wheat (Weizen) and rye (Roggen) flour, and

Vollkornbrot (Schwarzbrot)
made from whole rye or rye-and-wheat grains that are cracked or rough-ground.

Many varieties, from medium-brown to very dark-brown.

Pumpernickel
a very heavy type of bread, very dark and with a very special taste.

Not only are the varieties of bread, rolls, pretzels, cakes and cookies immense, there are also large differences from town to town. Therefore, the best advice we can give is to go to the nearest German baker's shop and to try out what they have there — make your own discoveries in the aromatic realm of German bread.

Naturally, Germans do not like their bread plain — and here is where the sausages come into play. There are more than 1,500 different kinds of German sausage — raw, boiled, and smoked, seasoned in all sorts of ways, shaped in all kinds of forms.

Regional and local variety is immense, not only in recipes but also in names, so that here again the best advice is to make your own discoveries (don't hesitate to ask for a small quantity, such as "hundert Gramm" or "ein Viertelpfund" only). Here are the most important kinds of sausage:

Mettwurst (ground pork sausage)
coarse, medium and fine
Leberwurst (liverwurst)
pork or veal, coarse and fine
Blutwurst (blood sausage)
meat (pork) and blood
Fleischwurst (bologna)
beef, pork and veal, to be fried or grilled
Bratwurst
pork sausage for frying, normal size or very small
Wiener Würstchen — wieners

Road and Rail Traffic

"Public transportation is fine in Germany — but driving... terrible, nerve-racking!" That is what Americans usually say about the traffic situation over here. "I returned my rented car on the second day because I saw my life endangered by those horrid drivers," an American tourist told an interviewer just recently.

The Speed Shock

The greatest shock to Americans is the speed at which Germans drive. With few exceptions, there is no speed limit on the big freeways, or Autobahns (which are toll-free). There is only a "recommended speed" of 130 km/h (approx. 80 miles/h); most drivers nowadays don't go much over this limit, but some do, and they are the ones who terrify the slow drivers on the left (passing) lanes of the Autobahns, "tail-gating" and sometimes even flashing their lights (which is illegal).

On highways and secondary roads outside towns, the speed limit is 100 km/h (62 mi.), in towns 50 km/h and sometimes, on larger streets, 60 km/h (look for the signs).

All those speed limits are not so strictly enforced as in the United States. There are radar controls, but obviously not enough, and the fines imposed are too low to really frighten drivers out of going 10 or 20 km above the limit. Only in extreme cases is the driver's license taken away.

Ever since oil has become such a valuable commodity, however, gasoline prices in Germany (always much higher than in the U.S.) soared, too. Fast driving has become very expensive, and there's hope that enough drivers are beginning to feel the pinch and are slowing down. People are also driving less kilometers per car than they used to. This and the fact that wearing seat-belts has become mandatory here has made for lower accident figures recently, in spite of a still growing number of cars.

Dense Traffic

Most Germans love their cars, as you can easily see from the good shape in which they keep them. Germans also keep their cars for more years than Americans usually do. To the younger generation, owning a car is now almost a matter of course, but their parents had to get used to it. Just imagine that back in 1952 there were only 945,000 passenger cars in West Germany, now there are 23 million! For a country as small as West Germany this means that in spite of the many new roads traffic density is now much higher than, for instance, in the U.S.

Except for the Autobahns, most overland roads are narrower here than in America; some have high crowns, dangerous curves, and cobblestone pavement which is treacherous when wet. The congested maze of European city streets presents many problems to the American driver.

They are full of "no-entry" and "one-way street" signs, and sometimes you may find yourself going in a circle several times before finding the one little street that leads to your destination.

The variety of vehicles is much greater in Germany than in the States. Not only must you watch out for bicycles, motorcycles, busses, and extra-large trucks, but there are also great varieties among ordinary passenger cars. As the car tax is fixed according to the cylinder capacity, some smaller cars are not strong enough to accelerate as quickly as the normal American car. This is especially noticeable in passing maneuvers, which take more time and therefore are more dangerous.

There is also a difference in the behavior at stoplights. When the red light changes to yellow, meaning "stay put until the green appears," most German drivers view it as a preliminary "go" signal and shoot off, sometimes barely missing those traveling in the other direction where the light is changing to red and who seem to understand their yellow light not as "stop" or "clear the intersection" but as "hurry up or you'll have to stop."

A flashing yellow light always means "Caution." Unless there's a green arrow pointing their way, cars waiting at a red light are not allowed to turn right, as is sometimes the case in America. Also pedestrians in Germany must wait for their green light before crossing even if there is apparently no traffic.

Drunken driving is a felony under German law, as is leaving the scene of an accident, passing illegally, making U-turns on Autobahns, and several other traffic offenses.

It is also important to know that children under 12 years of age must ride in the back seats of cars here.

Keep Alert!

Our general advice to American drivers in Germany: learn the traffic rules well, maintain a sufficient interval, and try to stay out of situations that call for fast braking. Watch out for zebra-stripe crosswalks, where pedestrians have the absolute right of way, and remember that at unmarked intersections traffic coming from the right has the right of way. Don't be overcautious either, but never take driving easy over here. Always keep alert!

Car Insurance, License Plates, and "Fahrschule"

Liability insurance is obligatory.

The first group of letters on the license plate stands for the town or district.

Beware of "Fahrschule" cars!

Who ran into whom? That's the big question! Liability insurance is obligatory for all car owners in Germany. The car tax grows with the cylinder capacity.

In Germany, a car keeps the same license plate as long as it is registered with the local traffic authority. If the owner moves to another district, he has to register the car at the new place.

The first group of letters on the plate stands for the town or district (HH = Hansestadt Hamburg, M = Munich, etc.). Anybody wishing to obtain a driver's license in Germany has to go to an autho-rized driver's school (Fahrschule). Then, he has to undergo a written and a driving test with the traffic authorities. The license is good for a lifetime.

Beginners sometimes put a little sign in their rear windows to warn the fellow drivers: "Anfänger!"

Another Traffic Hazard: Bicycles

Bicycle Paths Are not for Walking, nor for Parking!

Americans coming to Germany will soon notice that the bicycle population is much greater over here than in the States, and that one sees people from two to ninety-two on bikes. Therefore, American drivers and pedestrians alike must be on their toes and should observe a few simple tips:

Pedestrians must be careful not to mistake the bicycle path for a sidewalk. In Germany, quite often these special lanes are in better shape than the sidewalks, but don't walk on them — you might get hit from the rear. Also look before crossing one.

Car drivers must always watch out for bicycles before making a right turn around a corner. Also, when passing cyclists, keep a safe distance and remember that they are not always aware of the traffic rules!

It is forbidden to park a car on a bicycle path, but the sides of many sidewalks can be used for parking if they have special signs.

Not all of these cyclists know the traffic rules... therefore, take care!

Watch for bicycles before making a right turn around a street corner.

When Driving in Germany ...

Don't bump that bumper!

On the Autobahn: no passing on the right (except in slow lanes)

..don't bump that bumper

Germans can be very touchy about their cars. German courts have decided that one must absolutely avoid even touching another car when maneuvering in and out of parking spaces, let alone bump its bumper. German bumpers are not made especially strong; also there is no standard height required for bumpers as in the States. So the first rule in parking is DON'T BUMP THAT BUMPER!!!

...and don't lose your patience

Sunday drivers are fine — on the scenic route — but not on the Autobahn, and especially not in the passing lane. In Germany, as in the States, the left lane of a two-lane freeway is for passing only, and the right lane is for driving. It is generally forbidden to pass on the right on Autobahns; only when traffic is proceeding in both lanes and the left lane is moving not faster than 60 km/h or has come to a standstill, are the cars in the right lane allowed to move ahead, with utmost care, at a speed that does not exceed that of the left lane by more than 20 km/h.

May I Help You?

The following phrases may be helpful to know if you have car trouble or if you wish to help a German driver on the road (in case of accidents with injured persons, German law obliges you to help!):

Haben Sie eine Panne? = Are you having car trouble?
Kann ich Ihnen helfen? = May I help you?
Ja, das ist sehr freundlich von Ihnen! = Yes, that is very kind of you.
Der Wagen springt nicht an = The car won't start.
Soll ich anschieben? = Do you want me to push?
Könnten Sie ihn mit anschieben? = Could you help push it?
Wir müssen das Auto anschleppen = We must tow the car.
Haben Sie ein Abschleppseil? = Do you have a tow rope?
Vielen Dank! = Thank you very much!

Anschieben" — to push a car

Emergency Calls on the Autobahn

In case of a breakdown on the Autobahn, look for the little arrows near the top of the white posts lining the road. They'll lead you to the nearest emergency call box. These boxes are located every 1 1/2 to 3 kilometers along the Autobahns. To use, merely lift the handle; the autobahn superintendent's office will answer. Most of the operators speak English, and if they don't they will connect you with someone who does. Describe your problem, and help will be on the way in minutes.

What Does "Kriechspur" Mean?

Seitenstreifen nicht befahrbar!

"Soft Shoulders!"

Driving on hilly sections of the Autobahn, you may see the word "Kriechspur" once in a while. It means "creeping lane" and denotes an extra lane on the right intended especially for slow-moving trucks, which can only "creep" uphill and would otherwise hold up faster vehicles which can make the elevation more easily.

Sometimes, there are German explanations under the "Attention!" signs which foreigners may find hard to understand. Here are some translations:

Seitenstreifen nicht befahrbar — soft shoulders

Seitenwind — side wind

Fahrbahnschäden — damaged road surface

Rauch — smoke

Baustelle auf 15 km — construction lot for 15 km

If you wish to make a short stop on the Autobahn, you may drive into one of the parking places along the road which are announced by a sign that shows a white "P" on blue background. The sign "Rastplatz bitte sauberhalten" means "Please keep the rest area clean." The word "Raststätte" stands for the large restaurant-gas station complexes on the Autobahns.

Before complicated traffic intersections, there are sometimes signs indicating several directions with the words "Bitte einordnen!" above them. This means "Please move into the proper lane!"

"Einfädeln" means "to thread in," i.e. to carefully merge into a traffic lane.

If your car breaks down, your first obligation is to warn oncoming traffic. Put warning lights or triangles at a sufficient distance from the car to enable drivers approaching from the rear to react in time.

At a German Gas Station

Volltanken, bitte!

In gas stations offering full service, the attendant who cleaned your window, checked the air pressure, etc. expects a tip.

You need not speak much at a self-service gas station (SB = Selbstbedienung), but at other stations you may have to use some German words:

To have your tank filled up, say "Volltanken, bitte!" You can also ask for 10, 20, etc. liters of gas = "zehn, zwanzig Liter Benzin." Roughly, one gallon equals nearly four liters; therefore, ten gallons of gas would be about forty liters. Regular gasoline is called "Normal" in German, ethyl is "Super" or "Extra."

To have the air pressure in the tires checked, ask for "Reifendruck prüfen" or, more colloquial, "Luft nachsehen." Air pressure is not measured in pounds per square inch here but in "bar" (formerly AT). For example, 28 PSI is 1.9 bar, and 30 PSI is 2.1 bar.

Oil is "Öl" in German; the battery, "die Batterie;" the tire, "der Reifen."

die Tankstelle — gas station
das Ersatzteillager — parts store
die Reparaturwerkstatt — repair shop
der LKW, Lastkraftwagen — truck
der PKW, Personenkraftwagen — ordinary car

Taxi Language

A cab or taxi is called "die Taxe" or "das Taxi" in German. The cab driver is "der Taxifahrer." Indicating the destination of your ride, you may say: "Ich möchte zum Bahnhof, bitte" (to the station, please) or "zur Hauptstrasse, bitte" or "zur Kaserne, bitte!" (to the main street, to the barracks).

If you want him to stop, say "Bitte, halten Sie hier!"

Taxi rates vary from town to town. Within one area, the rate may vary depending on the time of the day, the number of passengers and the luggage transported. The number of passengers a driver may take is limited by law.

Make certain you have enough Deutsche Mark in small denominations. Taxi drivers will probably accept dollar bills, too, but at a much less favorable rate than usual, to make up for the time and gasoline needed to travel to a bank or currency exchange.

A 10 % tip is customary.

Taking a cab (eine Taxe nehmen)

Zum Bahnhof, bitte!

Subways, Streetcars, and Buses

Don't go through the subway gate without a ticket — those who do have a subscription ticket.

Living in a German city, you will soon notice that you can save time, gas, and nerves by using public transportation. Berlin, Hamburg, and Munich have extensive subway systems, other cities have one or two subway lines. All have highly developed bus systems, and some still have streetcars.

Get to know the local public transportation system. There are variations from city to city in the prices, ticket zones, and in how tickets are bought and validated.

A New Yorker, used to paying his fare each time he uses the subway, may wonder what the German system is like when he sees that some people apparently buy a ticket while others simply walk through the open gate. The explanation is "Zeitkarten" (subscription tickets valid for a week, a month, etc.) which are used by regular customers. Never enter a subway without having a ticket — you may have to pay a fine. There are sometimes checks either in the trains themselves or at the exit gates. "Zeitkarten" are also used for streetcars and buses. In Hamburg, Munich, and in the Ruhr region a practical system has been introduced under which the same ticket is valid for all means of public transportation

— the subway, the city railway, street cars, buses, and even (in Hamburg) river boats and ferries.

Many subway stations only have ticket automats. Make sure, therefore, that you have enough coins to buy your ticket from an automat.

In the subway, streetcar, or bus, if there is no seat left and an elderly person comes in, well-behaved children or young people offer their seats, saying "Bitte, nehmen Sie meinen Platz" or simply "Bitte schön!" If a seat bears the sign "Schwerbeschädigte," this means it is reserved for invalids.

Der Bus, die Fahrkarte

die U-Bahn — subway /underground
die S-Bahn — city railway
die Strassenbahn — streetcar /tram
der Bus — bus
die Bushaltestelle — bus stop
die Fahrkarte — ticket
der Fahrplan — schedule

Riding the Train in Germany

Have you ever thought of traveling in Germany by train? The trains of the German Federal Railroads (Deutsche Bundesbahn, a government-operated organization) are fast, punctual, clean, comfortable and safe. Long-distance trains have good diners and sleeping cars. Special "Autoreisezüge" even carry their passengers' automobiles along. Here are a few tips.

Reading the Schedule

First the train schedule. In German train stations you'll find two large schedules, prominently posted. One is marked "Ankunft," the other "Abfahrt." It's the second, yellow one you'll be interested in. It gives destinations, times of departures and so on. (Small train schedules can also be bought at any German train station.)

There are several columns on the Abfahrt schedule, with the following headings:

Zeit (meaning "time of departure")

Zug Nr ("train" number)

Nach (meaning "to" — in other words, destination)

Gleis (track)
or Bahnsteig (platform)

Look down the "Nach" column for a train that's going where you are, at about the time you'd like to leave. Departure times are in the "Zeit" column; military time is used. Times of arrival are shown after the city of destination, in smaller numerals, in the "Nach" column.

The kind of train (not to be confused with class of travel) is important. There are four basic kinds:

Which Kind of Train?

1. Those listed in black type are Nahverkehrszüge, which are more or less "milk trains" that stop at nearly every fence post. These you'll want to avoid unless your trip is a short one. It's best to stick with the trains marked in red.

2. The first of the "red" trains is the Eilzug. These trains are marked by an "E" before the train number. It's advisable to take an Eilzug for trips of 50 kilometers or less.

3. Next is the D-Zug and D-City-Zug, marked with a "D" or "DC" before the train number. These trains are faster and make fewer stops than the "E"-trains, but for distances under 50 kilometers you pay a

bit extra — 3 marks, a so-called Zuschlag (supplement). You get a separate ticket for the Zuschlag, which you can buy with your regular ticket at the window, or from the conductor on the train (but this costs extra). D-City trains (first and second class) connect 73 German towns with the four main routes of the "Intercity" system explained in the next paragraph.

4. The fourth kind of train has an "IC" (for Intercity-Zug) or "TEE" (for Trans-Europa-Express) before the train number. These comfortable long-distance trains are very fast, and whiz through most smaller towns. But again, you pay extra for the fast service and comfort. The Zuschlag is 10 marks for 1st and 3 marks for 2nd class (including seat reservation — Platzkarte), and the 22 TEE trains (Trans-Europe-Expresses) have only first class. They bear fancy names such as "Rheingold," "Gambrinus," etc.

152 Intercity trains, which have both first and second class cars, link 47 major German cities all over the country at one-hour intervals between 7 a.m. and 11 p.m. The four main Intercity lines meet at Cologne, Dortmund, Hannover and Mannheim, with connections available, and as a rule pas-

sengers need only cross the platform to change trains.

The number in the last column of the departure schedule, "Gleis" or "Bahnsteig," shows which track or platform your train leaves from.

Departure schedules also have a number of symbols pertaining to trains, some of which are important. If there's any small print under the time in the "Zeit" column of the train you're interested in, it's best to inquire at "Information" (Auskunft). It probably has to do with times when the train will or will not run.

Several different symbols are used in the "Nach" column. Crossed knife and fork, as might be expected, means the train has a dining car — called Speisewagen. The symbol of a wine glass means that food and drink are available on the train, probably sold by vendors who wander through the cars.

A bed means, obviously, that the train has a sleeping car (Schlafwagen, wagon-lit). A smaller symbol, supposed to represent a couch, means that the train has a car or cars convertible for sleeping purposes, though these aren't regular sleeping cars.

Such cars are called „Liegewagen" (couchettes). You don't change clothes in these cars, sexes are not separated, and you get only a blanket and a pillow. The supplement is much cheaper than for a Schlafwagen. If you plan to use either a Schlafwagen or a Liegewagen, be sure to make a reservation when you get your ticket, especially in the holiday seasons.

If you have any question at all about your train, see Auskunft, Information. People in this office will go to great lengths to help you get where you're going.

Buying the Ticket

Buy your ticket at any window marked "Fahrkarten—Inland." Fahrkarte means "ticket." Inland means what you'd suppose. If you want a ticket to go outside Germany, go to a window marked "Ausland."

To ask for a ticket, simply say "nach ....., bitte" — wherever you're going. If you don't speak German, it might be best to write your destination on a slip of paper and show it to the person behind the window. German place names are tricky to pronounce, and the usual American pro-

nunciations are often radically different from the German.

If your ticket is to be one-way, add the word "einfach," which means literally "simple." If you want a round-trip, say "hin und zurück," which means "there and back." You can also say "Rückfahrkarte." (If you don't use the ticket for your return, incidentally, you can redeem it at the station.)

There are reductions for one-day round trips (Tagesrückfahrkarten) within 50 kilometers from your departure point. Sonderrückfahrkarten (special, reduced round trip tickets) are issued for weekend trips on "commercially interesting" routes, i.e. where it is profitable for the railroads.

Furthermore, there are all kinds of reductions for groups (two adults and one child already form a "mini-group") and favorable arranged tours. Large reductions (of usually 50 per cent) are possible for holders of a "Senioren-Pass" (for women over 60 and men over 65), a "Junioren-Pass" (for young people between 12 and 22), "Eurail" and "Interrail" passes. Inquire about these details at any larger train station where English-speaking personnel is sure to be available.

74

What about classes of trains? There are only two, first and second. The first is plushy and rather expensive. It's to be recommended only if you're feeling expansive or if you want to assure yourself a seat during a rush period. (But a cheaper way of doing this is to reserve yourself a second-class seat by means of a Platzkarte.) Second-class usually has leather seats, not plushy but fairly comfortable.

Checking Baggage

To check baggage at a station temporarily, go to a window marked with a whopper of a word: "Gepäckaufbewahrung." Gepäck means "baggage." Many stations now have lockers (Schließfächer). If you use these, be sure to pay the extra amount required if you plan to check your bag longer than the stated maximum.

To check baggage on your ticket, go to a window marked "Reisegepäck." (Reise means trip.) Of course it's simpler to carry your baggage with you, if you can handle it all.

A restaurant will usually be available in the station — often two: first and second class. They have nothing to do with the class of ticket you have; it's simply that the layout and fare of the first-class restaurant will be a bit fancier.

Larger train stations have facilities for everything from exchanging money to buying toothpaste. Many have automats that dispense such items as shaving cream, stockings, and candy bars.

About ten minutes before your train is due to depart, go to the platform.

Platforms and tracks are clearly marked by number. On your platform there's likely to be a sign giving the destination and time of departure of your train. Check this sign to confirm that you're where you should be.

German trains usually run on schedule. Late trains are announced over a P. A. system, and there's the usual amount of garbling normally connected with train announcements. When you hear an announcement, listen for your destination, the train number, or the time of departure. The expression in German for being late is "Verspätung haben" — literally "to have lateness." If you can catch this word you may be able to tell how late your train will be. Of course, you can always ask someone on the platform. On small or medium-sized stations, the fast trains stop often for only one or two minutes. Only in the large towns are the stops a little longer.

Train Etiquette

Classes of cars are pretty prominently marked "1" or "2" so you'll know which is which. Check also to see whether your car is a Raucher (smoker) or a Nichtraucher (nonsmoker). Some cars are half and half.

Some overland trains combine cars with different destinations for part of the trip, which may be disconnected at a certain station and added to other trains. Therefore, you ought to check whether the car bears the right destination on the outside before entering it; there are also signs in the cars themselves. If you have a "Platzkarte" with a car number, look for the "Wagenstandanzeiger" (a graphic plan showing the order of the cars in the train) on the platform to see where your car will stop.

Train etiquette calls for you to greet the occupants in the compartment upon entering and to ask whether a seat is occupied before you sit down. The usual

(continued on page 76)

Some Railroad Words in Short

Train travel in Germany is simple if you know a few terms. The train schedule (Fahrplan) is easy to find in the station (Bahnhof). It is marked with "Ankunft" (arrival) and "Abfahrt" (departure). "Zeit" means time of departure; "Nach" means to, i. e. the destination; "Zug Nr." is the train number; "Gleis" is track; and "Bahnsteig" is platform. Trains printed in red and marked with "D," "DC," "IC" or "TEE" are the fastest.

"Fahrkarten" means tickets. Simply say "nach ..." — wherever you are going. For one-way, add "einfach," roundtrip is "hin- und zurück" or "Rückfahrkarte." For D, DC, IC and TEE trains you pay a supplement (Zuschlag), with the last one being exclusively first class (erste Klasse). To reserve a seat, get yourself a "Platzkarte." "Sonderrückfahrkarten" are reduced weekend tickets valid only on certain routes.

"Gepäckaufbewahrung" is the place where you can check baggage at a station temporarily. "Gepäck" means baggage. To check baggage on your ticket, go to a window marked "Reisegepäck." "Annahme" is where they accept your baggage, "Ausgabe" is where you get it back. A porter is called "Gepäckträger" in German. Lockers are called "Schließfächer" in German.

Riding the Train in Germany   (continued)

question is, "Ist dieser Platz frei?" It's also common to say goodbye to other occupants when you leave.

Your ticket will probably be punched once while you're on the train. The conductor may ask for "Fahrkarten," or he may use the expression "Ist noch jemand zugestiegen?" which means "Has anyone here boarded since tickets were last checked?" Normally you show your ticket only once.

German trains, like other European trains, have no drinking water. (The water from the faucet in the lavatory is not drinkable.) If you're thirsty, try to catch a vendor selling bottled drinks.

As for restroom facilities, you'll find them at the end of the car. There are no separate facilities for men and women. The sign on the door will say "Toilette." The sign near the handle of the door of the Toilette will tell you whether the room is occupied (besetzt) or free (frei). In modern trains, a wash room (Waschraum) with a hand basin but without toilet is to be found near the Toilette.

Except for TEE and IC trains, stops are not announced in the train, but over loudspeakers in the station. It's a good idea to

have checked the schedule and know about when you'll arrive at your destination. Stations themselves are pretty well marked with large signs. "Hbf" stands for Hauptbahnhof (main station). Larger cities will have several smaller train stations, sometimes marked Süd, Nord, West and Ost (south, north, west, east). Normally you'll want to get off at the main station.

Gute Reise!

Reduced Fare Plans

In addition to the special tickets, etc. described in the preceding chapter, the following reduced fare plans are particularly interesting (rates as of the beginning of 1980):

Germain Rail Tourist Card: An unlimited mileage ticket that takes holders anywhere in West Germany. The card also gives holders free or reduced-rate travel by bus or boat on selected routes. Valid for nine days it costs about DM 200 for second class, for 16 days DM 280. First class tickets cost DM 280 for nine days and

DM 390 for 16 days. Ordering such a card at a small station will take a couple of days.

Tramper Monats Ticket: Offers unlimited second class travel for persons 19—22 and students up to age 25 on German trains up to one month. It costs DM 198. A passport photo is required.

Group Travel: Reduced rates for six or more passengers (up to 140). Lowest rates are during low season and nonholiday periods. Apply at least seven days before your departure date.

Family Pass: This DM 198 pass offers half-price travel on German trains for one year to all members of one family.
Children must be under 18, unmarried and living in the same household. If an adult is traveling, at least two persons must go together; but one child can travel alone.

U.S. School Trips: Special one- to seven-day trips for American Dependent Schools in the Federal Republic of Germany. For detailed information, phone Herr Muscheid or Herr Kugies of the German Rail Travel Service at Frankfurt (0611) 265-5425 /5565.

Reprinted and adapted from EurArmy

The Mail and the Phone

You've probably seen its bright yellow deposit boxes and trucks with their distinctive post horn symbol; maybe you've seen or ridden its yellow buses, which carry both mail and passengers. The German Federal Postal System (Bundespost) is pretty hard to ignore; its facilities are everywhere.

Multitude of Services

Besides performing what Americans think of as normal postal services (and operating its buses), the Bundespost also:

— owns and operates West Germany's telephone and telegraph systems (facilities for both are available at local post offices) as well as the Telex and Datex services

— owns or controls the equipment for West Germany's radio and television networks

— offers banking services — both savings and checking accounts (through local post offices)

— offers subscriptions to newspapers and magazines.

Following are some tips on how to use the local German post office.

Telegrams

First, telegrams. Except for the fact that you send them from the post office rather than Western Union, the system is much the same as in the States. You merely put your message on a form, available at the post office, and take it to the counter. You can also phone in a telegram.

A mailgram, or letter telegram, is called "Brieftelegramm" in German.

Telephone

Telephone calls to anywhere in the world can be placed at a German post office. Simply go to the counter marked "Telefon" or "Fernsprecher" and give the operator the number you want. She'll place the call and direct you to a booth to take it. You may be asked to pay a deposit before the call; the final bill you pay afterward.

More than likely, however, you'll do your public phoning from a (Bundespost-owned) booth. There are two kinds of booths. One is for local calls only. A single call costs two 10-Pfennig pieces. If you want to call German information, the word to look for on the cover of the phone book is "Auskunft." Most information operators speak some English.

The other kind of booth phone is for local and long distance calls. It is larger and has coin slots for 50-Pfennig and 1-Mark pieces as well as a 10-Pfennig slot. Using it you can call anywhere in Germany, and even abroad from some phone booths. You have to know the area code prefix (Vorwahl), of course, which you can get from a list placed on the wall next to the phone or from Auskunft. For a long-dis-

tance call you deposit your 20 Pfennige, dial straight through, begin talking, and then drop in more money, each time the sign "Sprechzeit zu Ende" (speaking time is up) lights. If you want a distant military number, you dial the area code first, then the military prefix of the area, then your number.

During the hours 6 p. m. to 8 a. m. there is a cheaper rate for direct-dial long-distance calls. The night rate also applies on Saturdays and Sundays as well as on most German holidays.

For private phones, the cost per call unit is 23 Pfennigs. After 1982, everywhere in West Germany and West Berlin (already introduced in some places) the duration of a call unit for local calls will be limited to eight minutes (twelve minutes for the night rate). — More about telephoning on page 81.

Buying Stamps

As a rule, stamps can only be bought in a post office or from stamp vending machines outside post offices or elsewhere in the town. Frequently, shops selling picture postcards also have stamps available.

Letter and Card Service

Letter and card service is pretty much like the American (but faster).

Normal letters to German destinations and also all letters and cards to European countries, including Turkey and Russia, automatically go airmail without additional charge.

Airmail letter rates to other foreign countries vary. It's best to check at the counter. There are also special rates for printed matters (Drucksachen).

You can, of course, send a letter or postcard (or Päckchen, discussed later) by registered mail. Just say, "Einschreiben, bitte." And you can have a letter or postcard sent by special delivery (Eilboten).

Postleitzahlen

Germany, too, has zip-code numbers (Postleitzahlen). A booklet listing them is available at the post office. In the address the German zip code comes before the name of the city. If you know the number of the delivery post office (used in large communities only), put it after the name of the city. This what the letter address should look like:

Herrn (Frau or Fräulein)
Dr. H. Schmidt
Schulzstraße 35

5300 Bonn 1

Note that the name of the street comes before the street number. The return address should be written into the left upper corner of the envelope's front. — For international mail between most European countries, it is sufficient to add the letters used to identify the "nationality" of cars to the zip code: D 5300 Bonn. And don't omit the "n" in "Herrn."

For c/o you write "per Adr." in German letter addresses, or, for persons living with a German family, "bei" (bei Schmidt). "zu Hd. von" or "z. Hd." means Attn. (Mr. X).

Parcels

There are two classes of package, the "Paket" and the "Päckchen." The Paket is a normal package, sent by parcel post methods, the rate depending on the weight and the distance sent. In addition to the address on the package itself, a separate card (Paketkarte) must be filled out. Each ordinary parcel is insured up to 500.00 DM. Additional insurance may be had for a fee (called Wertgebühr). The delivery service charges a fee for each package delivered, unless the sender has paid this charge at the time of mailing.

If your package is small, ask if it will go as a Päckchen. A Päckchen is forwarded like a parcel, but at a much cheaper rate. No Paketkarte is required for it. For Päckchen to foreign countries you will, however, have to fill out a small green customs declaration.

If you want rush service on a package, send it as a "Schnellsendung" (within the Federal Republic) or as a "dringendes Paket" (to foreign countries).

Postal Money Orders

The "Zahlkarte" is the pale blue form used for paying money into a postal checking account (Postscheckkonto).

The pink "Postanweisung" is used if the money is to be paid in cash directly to an individual or firm.

The "Auslandspostanweisung" is an international money order. You pay German marks, and the recipient of the payment receives cash in the currency of his country.

Eurocheques, American Express traveler's cheques, and DM traveler's cheques of German financial institutions may be cashed at all post offices with the "ec" symbol during normal hours (bring your passport along).

Large German post offices are so set up that the various counters are specialized with regard to their services; each has a sign over it telling what it handles.

If you have any questions about how to use German post office services, ask at the counter. There will usually be someone on hand who speaks some English. Or, if you know some German, get a little yellow booklet, called "Postgebührenheft," at the post office. It contains detailed information.

For Stamp Enthusiasts:

Stamp collectors who want to make sure that they get all new German stamps can subscribe and have the new stamps sent every three months. Pick up and fill out a form at the post office, or write to:

Versandstelle für Sammlermarken
Mainzer Landstr. 187—189
6000 Frankfurt 1

or to:

Versandstelle für Sammlermarken
Goethestraße 2
1000 Berlin 12.

More About Telephoning

of the U. S. phone system does not exist in Germany. The German telephone network is fully automatic so that you can dial all your inland calls yourself.

Calling from the Hotel

Many an American tourist in Germany gets a shock when he's confronted with his hotel telephone bill. 30 Dollars for a direct 3-minute call from Germany to the U.S. is considered "normal" by a leading Hamburg hotel (although it is less in smaller hotels). German hotel managers insist that their high telephone rates are no "rip-off" but that they need the money to make up for the costs of installing and maintaining the complicated self-dialing equipment.

Looking for "Operator?"

Except for company and hotel phone operators, the ever-present, helpful operator

Calling Abroad

You can also dial calls to some 50 countries outside Germany directly from any private phone, many hotel phones, and from a few public pay phones (you will find such special booths, marked with a green sign, at the airports, for instance).

First of all, you dial the country code, followed immediately by the code for the desired local network area and lastly the subscriber's call number. Accounting is performed in charge units of DM 0.23 according to the duration of the call.

A self-dialed night call (midnight to noon, daily) to anywhere in the U.S. except Hawaii and Alaska will cost you DM 36,34 for six minutes. A self-dialed day call (noon to midnight, daily) is DM 44,16 for the same length call. Calling from Germany to the U.S. is over twice as expensive as calling the other way.

Note: if you have a private phone in Germany, your monthly phone bill will indicate, in the column "Anzahl der Gebühreneinheiten," not the number of phone calls you made but the number of charge units (which is one per local call but may be 10 or 20 or more for long-distance calls). Twenty charge units per month are included in the minimum monthly fee.

All the country codes and the most frequently used area codes are to be found in the little yellow book that comes with the telephone directory. If you have any questions about numbers or codes, ring Information (usually, the line is busy and you must wait!): for national trunk calls: 118 or 0118, for international trunk calls: 00118.

If you need the help of an operator after all, call 010 for inland and 0010 for abroad.

No "Special" Calls

As there is normally no operator involved in the German telephone system, there are also no person-to-person calls possible, no collect calls, no credit card calls, and no calls can be charged to another number.

On the Phone

Answering a phone call, Germans do not say "Hello" but give their family name.

"Schmidt & Co., guten Tag!" "Könnte ich bitte Herrn Meier sprechen?"

The sign "Fasse dich kurz!" in phone booths means "Make it short!"

Telephone Language

When answering the phone, whether at home or in the office, it is customary in Germany to give one's family name. Asking to be transferred to someone else, the caller may say, for instance: "Guten Tag, hier ist Meier, könnte ich bitte Herrn Müller sprechen?"

Company operators often answer calls with an additional "Guten Tag" or "Grüss Gott." When transferring a call, they will say: "Moment (Augenblick), bitte" or "ich verbinde" (I'll transfer you).

"Bitte, bleiben Sie am Apparat!" means "hold on, please!" For "Sorry, wrong number" the German equivalent is "Entschuldigung, falsch verbunden" or "ich habe mich verwählt."

Ending a telephone conversation, most Germans say "Auf Wiederhören!" It means "hope to hear you again," just as "Auf Wiedersehen" means "hope to see you again."

The official word for telephone is "Fernsprecher," but everyone says "Telefon." The word for phone booth is "die Telefonzelle."

Emergency Calls

In most German communities, the police phone number for any emergency is 110, and the fire department and emergency first-aid service is usually reached by calling 112.

Some public telephone booths are equipped with a lever device that puts your emergency call right through with no need to dial or deposit coins.

Some words you may need when reporting an emergency:

fire — Feuer

hold-up — Überfall

accident — Unfall

with injured persons — mit Verletzten

burglary — Einbruch

German Isn't That Tough!

"I'd like to air a grievance," I said to Fritz, my German friend, the other day.

"And that is?" he asked.

"I think that the Germans shouldn't always contend that their language is so difficult."

"I beg your pardon!"

"I said I don't think German is so hard!"

"Na, sowas! (aghast). How can you say such a thing? Why the Germans themselves make mistakes even. And the grammar! (eyes cast upwards in awe). So-o-o difficult. First off, there's the problem of distinguishing between "mir" and "mich." And then there's "der, die, das." How could a foreigner possibly remember all that? And capitalization. And (breathless)..."

"Stop, stop, stop — bitte."

"Bitte?!"

Please excuse me, dear reader, for interrupting him so abruptly, but this heated discussion on the difficulties of learning German could go on for hours! "Die deutsche Sprache ist eine schwere Sprache," my German friend Fritz claims.

He is not alone; most Germans entertain the very same thought. And I as an English speaking person, an American, disagree. Is the German language really s o terribly difficult? Is it impossible for a foreigner to learn it, at least half way fluently? I don't think so and here are a few of my reasons why.

In the first place, an English speaking person attempting to learn German unknowingly has put a few rounds of the battle behind him. Why? Because English and German are blood brothers. Both are divergences of the so-called Indo-European language, a prehistoric tongue from which many, many others have emerged. Anglo-Saxon, the first form of English, was a Germanic dialect. This was later strongly influenced by French.

Being two peas from the same linguistic pod, there should then be a great similarity. The beginner doesn't have to delve deeply into the complexities of German before he begins to meet some very familiar looking words — der Arm, die Hand, der Ball, das Gold, der Finger. Philologists call these "perfect cognates" because the meaning and spelling are exactly the same. Nor does the beginner have to be a genius to see the similarity of the "near cognates" — die Mutter, der Vater, das Bier, der Mann, die Maus, das Haus. You'll be meeting hundreds of these two types of words throughout your study of German.

Sooner or later you'll stumble on another type of "old friend," and then a second, and a third and a fourth. Why, there seems to be no end of them. I'm talking about the Fremdwörter, the "foreign words," so called because they have crept into the German language through the centuries from other languages, without undergoing much "Germanization." Just a flip of the tongue to give the word "a German touch," and you have die Explosion, die Nation, die Information, die Position, das Element, direkt, absolut, der Doktor (of Latin extraction); das Chaos, die Atmosphäre, das Drama, die Politik (Greek); das Manöver, die Parade, der Offizier, die Armee, der Moment (French); der Moskito (Spanish); die Arie, das Stakkato (Italian); der Sport, der Flirt, boxen, der Jazz, das Handikap (English).

If a German stumbles over a Fremdwort, don't smirk; some of the more difficult ones like Psychologie or Meteorologie are really hundred-dollar tongue twisters. In English, these same words present less of a problem. The American is more apt to glibly rattle them off; in a way his whole language is "fremd." Several times in German history, attempts have been made to 'rout out these words — without much success. A word of warning though; although usually the meaning of these Fremdwörter correspond, once in a while one trips you up. One good example that comes to my mind is the German "sensibel," which has nothing in common with the English conception of the word. A sensible Frau ist not a sensible woman, but a sensitive woman!

Now, I'm afraid, the similarity ends. But there's another trick to learning the language, which German itself offers by its very make-up and which lends it a particular charm. German is a picture language. And the Germans themselves don't even realize it. As a child uses building blocks to construct houses and tunnels and buildings, German makes use of its simple words by putting two or three together — but there always remains a logical thread between the original word and the new.

One of my very favorite of these words is the German for skunk. This animal's most obvious characteristic is that it stinks. The Germans evidently thought so, too. They named it a Stinktier (Tier = animal). But what might they call a thimble? In your mind's eye picture a thimble on your fin-

86

ger. What does it look like? A hat perhaps? Sure — thimble in German is Fingerhut, a finger hat. The psychology of this word goes even deeper, for the English hat (an Anglo-Saxon word, and remember that Anglo-Saxon was a Germanic dialect) and the German Hut derive from an old word "huot," which in one sense means protection. A hat protects your head from the outside elements, a thimble protects your finger from the prick of the needle. And further, eine Hütte (hut) is a little house giving shelter. To be "auf der Hut" means to be on your guard.

Because of the picturesqueness of German words, they can be easily remembered and a basic vocabulary is built up rather quickly. Here are a few more picture words:

Volksmund	people's/mouth (vernacular)
Arbeitgeber	work/giver (employer)
Menschenfresser	human being/eater (cannibal)
Menschenfreund	human being/friend (philanthropist)
Blutarmut	blood/poverty (anemia)
Schirmherr	schirmen: to protect (patron)
Fallschirm	fall/umbrella (parachute)
Durchschnitt	through/cut (average)
Ausflug	out/fly (excursion)
Bildhauer	picture/cutter (sculptor)
Standbild	stand/picture (statue)
Neugier	new/eagerness, avidity (curiosity)

But there's still another possibility of word construction. This time your tools are — prefixes. Now, this sounds pretty dull — until you see how it is done. By adding various prefixes (for instance, be-, ent-, aus-, in-, auf-, über-) to one basic word, whole new word groups are opened up — but here again, no matter how diverse or abstract, if you try you can still literally "see" the tie-in with the root. Let me show you the verb führen (to lead):

Young Bob plans to take out (ausführen) his girl friend Sally one evening. He is well-liked and the leader (Anführer) of his gang. Up to now he has never been introduced (einführen) to Sally's parents. He tries to behave very well (sich gut aufführen). While waiting for Sally, Bob and her parents chitchat about this and that, his studies which he plans to pursue (fortführen), and then about trade, importing (einführen) and exporting (ausführen.) The young couple plans that evening to see a performance (Aufführung) of a play. Later that evening he tells her how alluring (verführerisch) she looks. They plan to marry, but up to now they cannot talk her father into the idea. In secret they talk about a plan they are going to carry out (durchführen). They will simply elope (entführen).

Many Americans have said to me that they think German is a "funny" language. They don't mean this at all in a derogatory sense. Nor do I, when I say German has a certain simplicity, naiveness, and humor quite lacking in English. Knowing this, one can understand all the better why some Germans think English is a bit "sober."

Acquisitions From the English

It is impossible in one short article to illustrate all the quaintnesses of German, but let me, as an example, introduce a particular friend of mine. I don't quite know what to call him, for "he" is not really a he, or feminine or even neuter. He is a strange little character that runs around doing all sorts of things that no one else wants to do. He opens doors and closes them, he even sits down for whole groups, to mention only two of his many duties. He does have a name though — "man." To go back to my two illustrations: in English "a door is opened or closed," but in German this strange little "mother's helper" goes to work — "man macht die Tür auf" or "zu," or "man setzt sich" and a hundred people sit down. In English this "man" is usually translated, if at all possible, by "one" or "you" or even "it."

No mention has been made yet of one subject, a subject which surely only a grammarian could love, namely grammar. And with reason. It is too vast. But grammar is a necessary evil. How could you, for instance, understand the insides of a car if you have not first taken it apart nut for bolt? Memorizing scads of rules is no fun. But once the rules of German grammar have been learned (there are really not too many of them and they are pretty much kept, contrary to English which only seems to "make 'em to break 'em"), the game may not have been won but a touchdown surely has been scored.

I'd like to point out just one more thing before closing, a real booby-trap which the beginner constantly falls into head over heels: translating idiomatic phrases from one language into the other. Sometimes it works, but other times — well, just beware! One evening at a very elegant cocktail party, a young American lady said to a distinguished guest with whom she was holding a conversation, "Wenn Sie nichts an haben, dann kommen Sie vorbei." Dead silence, for this seemingly innocent remark "to come on over, when you've nothing on" proved a real conversation stopper. "Nichts anhaben" conveys in German unfortunately only one meaning — the state of undress!

I hope with these few illustrations and tips I've succeeded in making my point that German is not impossible to learn. Over 70 million Germans speak German, and they can't all be geniuses!

Carolyn LaRocque

German has taken over many words from English, but sometimes the meaning has changed. Here are some of the more recent acquisitions (with the German gender of the nouns in parentheses):

Band (jazz band) (f)	Killer (m)
Beat (m)	Live (broadcast)
Bestseller (m)	Make up (n)
Boss (m)	Mid-life crisis (f)
Comeback (n)	Outsider (m)
Computer (m)	Paperback (n)
Container (m)	Party (f)
Countdown (m)	Pipeline (f)
Design (n)	Playboy (m)
Disc Jockey (m)	Public Relations (f)
Do-it-yourself	Publicity (f)
Drink (m)	Sex (m)
Entertainer (m)	Show (f)
Fairplay (n)	Sit-in (n)
Feature (n)	Song (m)
Festival (n)	Story (f)
Gag (joke) (m)	Teach-in (n)
Happening (n)	Team (n)
Hit (musical) (m)	Teenager (m)
Hobby (n)	Thriller (m)
Image (n)	Trend (m)
Job (m)	Understatement (n)

Reading German Signs

Direction signs are good and practical —
as long as you can understand them...
Here are a few translations of German
signs that you may find useful to know:

Achtung!	Attention!
Ausfahrt	Exit (for cars)
Ausfahrt freihalten	Don't block the driveway
Ausgang	Exit
Auskunft	Information
Bissiger Hund	Beware of Dog (Dog bites)
Bitte klingeln	please ring
Bitte nicht berühren	Do not touch
Drücken	Push (door)
Einfahrt	Entrance (for cars)
Eingang	Entrance
Fahrstuhl	Lift, Elevator
Flughafen	Airport
Geöffnet	Open

KEIN ZUTRITT

FAHRSTUHL ▷

AUSGANG ▶
◀ EINGANG

Vorsicht! Frisch gebohnert!

What does that mean?

Geschlossen	Closed
Hochspannung	High Tension
Kasse	Cashier
Keine Haftung	We take no responsibility, for objects deposited, etc.
Kein Zutritt	No Entry
Lebensgefahr!	Danger to Life!
Nichtraucher or Rauchen verboten	No smoking
Notausgang	Emergency Exit
Polizeiruf	Police Call
Reserviert	Reserved
Ruhe	Silence
Stadtmitte	City Center
Sprengstoff	Explosives
Tollwutgefahr	Danger: Rabid Animals in Area
ziehen	Pull (door)

Sprechen Sie Englisch?

Sprechen Sie Deutsch?

Here are a few phrases of "small talk" that you may find useful to know when opening a conversation with a German:

Sprechen Sie Englisch?
(Do you speak English?)

Verstehen Sie mich?
(Do you understand me?)

Ich spreche nur wenig Deutsch
(I speak only a little German)

Bitte, sprechen Sie etwas langsamer
(Please, speak a little more slowly)

Ich bin Amerikaner
(I am an American)

Woher kommen Sie?
(Where are you from?)

Ich komme aus...
(I come from ...)

Ich bin seit zehn Monaten in Deutschland
(I have been in Germany for ten months)

Mein Name ist ... (My name is ...)

And a little help if you want to make a date with a German girl:

Haben Sie heute nachmittag/abend schon etwas vor?
(Have you planned anything for this afternoon/evening?)

Haben Sie morgen abend Zeit?
(Are you free tomorrow night?)

Darf ich Sie zu einer Tasse Kaffee/zu einem Glas Wein/zu einem Drink/zum Essen/ins Kino/zum Tanzen/ einladen?
(May I invite you for a cup of coffee/for a glass of wine/for a drink/for dinner/for the movies/for dancing?

Ich hole Sie um... Uhr ab
(I will come to meet you at... o'clock)

Asking One's Way

Let's assume you have just arrived in a foreign German town. You wish to look up your father's elderly sister who still lives in the same house from which your father emigrated to the States 30 years ago. You know the name of the street, but unfortunately you do not have a map of the town (Stadtplan) with you. How can you ask your way in German?

Shortly after reaching the town, you see two housewives chatting on a street corner. You stop, roll down your window and ask, "Entschuldigen Sie bitte, können Sie mir wohl sagen, wie ich zur Neustädter Straße komme?" (Excuse me please, could you tell me how to get to the Neustädter Straße?)

"Neustädter Straße," the one repeats. She turns around and stretches out her arm in the direction in which your car is heading. "Immer geradeaus, junger Mann, ein ganzes Stück, und dann fragen Sie noch mal!" (Always straight ahead, young man, for quite a while, and then ask once more!)

"Danke sehr," (thank you), you say. She answers, "Bitte sehr!" (You're welcome).

After "a while," you come to a large crossing, where a policeman directs the traffic.

As he is in a big hurry, you ask him very shortly, "Zur Neustädter Straße, wie muß ich da fahren, bitte?" (To Neustädter Straße, where do I go, please?)

"Hier rechts," he answers, nodding to the right, "und dann die zweite Querstraße links!" (To the right here, and then take the second crossroad to the left.)

Again you do not forget your "Danke schön" and head for the right.

Alas, at the second crossing, there are two roads leading to the left! None of them is called "Neustädter Straße." Tentatively, you drive down the bigger one of the two until you see an old man. Again rolling down your window, you stop and ask, "Verzeihung; geht es hier zur Neustädter Straße?" (Excuse me, is this the right way to Neustädter Straße?)

The man nods, "Ja, da sind Sie richtig, dies ist die Verlängerung von der Neustädter Straße. Fahren Sie noch ein Stück weiter, dann kommt eine große Rechtskurve, und dann sind Sie auf der Neustädter Straße!" (Yes, you are on the right way, this is the extension of Neustädter Straße. Drive a little further, then there is a big curve to the right, and then you are on Neustädter

Straße.) Relieved, you say "Vielen Dank," and he answers, "Nichts zu danken!" (Don't mention it).

And two minutes later you stand before your father's house.

P.S. Foreigners often are confused by the fact that in the larger German towns several sections of one and the same street bear different names. After passing an intersection you may find, for instance, that "Neustädter Straße" suddenly is called "Adenauerallee," and several kilometers farther, what is apparently the same street now bears the name of "Bergstraße." On long roads, this may happen four or five or six times.

The House Floor Confusion

It's easy to mix up the house floors in Germany. What Americans call the first floor the Germans call the "Parterre" or "Erdgeschoss." Second floor would be "I. Stock" or "I. Etage" in German, third floor "II. Stock," etc.

Joe and Mary Go on a Sightseeing Tour (More Useful Words)

For a fine summer weekend, Joe and Mary have decided to go on a sight-seeing tour to Schönheim. Perhaps our little German vocabulary will help them to make the best of the trip.

On the map (Landkarte or simply Karte), Joe has found that Schönheim is only some 30 miles from where he is stationed. So, on a sunny morning, they get started, first a short stretch on the autobahn (die (Autobahn), then on a federal road (die Bundesstraße), and finally on a simple overland road (die Landstrasse). Schönheim, they have read in their "Guide Through Germany" (Führer durch Deutschland), is one of the old, romantic towns so typical of South Germany.

Approaching the town, they see from afar the high steeple (der Turm) of the church (die Kirche). The town is still surrounded by its ancient town wall (die Stadtmauer), which is reinforced by strong towers (die Türme). To get into the town, they have to drive through a narrow gate (das Tor); there is a special traffic sign (das Verkehrsschild) to show who has the right of way (die Vorfahrt) here. Schönheim still has cobblestone roads (das Kopfsteinpflaster), and most of them are one-way streets (die Einbahnstrasse), as they are very narrow. Joe thinks that they were certainly not built for such "boats" (der Strassenkreuzer) as his.

The town is very picturesque (sehr malerisch) with its many old half-timbered houses (die Fachwerkhäuser). If it were not for the traffic (der Verkehr), one might feel carried back to the Middle Ages (das Mittelalter). The market place (der Marktplatz) has a fine fountain (der Brunnen) in the middle. The big building facing it is the town hall (das Rathaus). It has a richly-ornamented front (eine reichverzierte Fassade).

Joe and Mary decide to look at (besichtigen) the church, the steeple of which they had seen from afar. Their travel guide says it is especially interesting. But in the maze of narrow streets they have difficulties finding it. They ask a woman who is coming their way: "Entschuldigen Sie bitte, wie kommen wir zur St. Martinskirche?" (Excuse me, please, how do we get to St. Martin's?) She turns round and points in the direction where Joe and Mary are heading: "Gehen Sie hier geradeaus, dann biegen Sie links ein, dann rechts, die schmale Gasse, und dann kommt gleich die Kirche!" (Go straight on here, then turn to the left, then to the right, the narrow lane, and then, soon after that, comes the church). They thank her ("Vielen Dank!") and follow her advice. Suddenly they stand in front of the large entrance (der Eingang) of St. Martin's. From the pointed arch (der Spitzbogen) they can see it is Gothic style (der gotische Stil). "What a huge church for such a small town," they think. The guide tells them that from the size of their churches you can see how important and rich those towns were in olden times.

Inside the church it is cool and quiet. The nave (das Kirchenschiff) is very high. One of the side altars (der Seitenaltar) is a famous work of art (ein berühmtes Kunstwerk), it is carved (geschnitzt) out of linden wood (aus Lindenholz). There is also a very old crucifix (das Kruzifix), which is of Romanesque style (der romanische Stil).

After leaving the church, Joe and Mary decide it is time for lunch (Zeit zum Mittagessen). There is a handwrought (handgeschmiedet) inn sign (Wirtshausschild) right in front of them, with a little bear in it. "Gasthaus zum Bären" is written over the entrance, together with the date "1735 A. D." They go in and sit down at one of the tables, invitingly laid with a white tablecloth. Joe asks for the menu (die Speisekarte) and orders "Zwei Bier!" right away. No translation needed.

P. S. Don't look for Schönheim on your map — it doesn't exist. Look for Dinkelsbühl, Nördlingen, Rothenburg instead.

Talking About the Weather

Der Schauer = shower

Der Regen = rain

Bedeckter Himmel = overcast sky

Wolkig = cloudy

Das Gewitter = thunderstorm

Das Wetter wird besser = the weather is going to be better

Es wird schön = it is going to be nice

Die Sonne kommt durch = the sun is coming through

Die Wolken reißen auf = the clouds are breaking up

Der Wind läßt nach = the wind is letting up

Schönes /gutes Wetter = fine /good weather

Es ist warm /heiß = it is warm /hot

ein klarer Tag = a clear day

Hochdruckgebiet = high-pressure area

Tiefdruckgebiet = low-pressure area

(More on German weather on page 132.)

"Es regnet schon wieder" (it's raining again). **"Es ist zu kühl für die Jahreszeit"** (it is too cool for the season.)

Frische Luft

It seems as if the Germans are especially "air-conscious." More than other people, they speak about the qualities of the air — be it "gute Luft, frische Luft, milde Luft, kalte Luft, feuchte Luft" or whatever.

A "Luftkurort" is a health resort where the air is considered particularly good — located in a forest, for instance.

Germans also speak of a "change of air" (Luftveränderung) if they mean that a change of climate will do their health good.

Of course, all this doesn't keep the Germans from having an absolute horror of drafts. Even on the hottest summer day when you're dying to feel a breeze (the Germans, too — outdoors!) someone will close either a window or a door because "es zieht" (there's a draft), and you'll catch a cold.

At the Beauty Parlor/Barber Shop — Beim Friseur

Have you yet had the fun of having your hair done at a German beauty parlor? If the answer is no, perhaps it is because you feel your "fractured" German might result in a Fiji-Island hairdo. This short vocabulary will help you. First the basics:

frisieren — to dress the hair

die Frisur — hairdo

der Friseur — barber, barber shop

der Friseursalon — beauty parlor

die Friseurin or Friseuse — beauty operator

When you enter the beauty shop, a young lady asks you "Bitte sehr?" (What can I do for you?)

"Waschen und legen, bitte!" (shampoo and set, please), you answer.

"Können Sie wohl zehn Minuten warten?" (Could you wait for about 10 minutes?) she asks. "Ja, ich warte" (yes, I'll wait), you say. "Bitte, nehmen Sie Platz" (please have a seat), she says and helps you take off your coat.

At last the waiting period is over. An operator seats you at a sink. She wraps a plastic cape around your shoulders, then hands you a small cloth. This is for your eyes, because in Germany usually one's hair is washed with the forehead pointed down toward the sink. The operator will want to know what kind of shampoo to use. Just tell her, "Ich habe fettiges (trockenes) Haar." (I have oily (dry) hair.)

"Wie soll ich Ihr Haar frisieren?" (How shall I set your hair?) she asks. The easiest, of course, would be to tell her, "wie es war" (do it like it was). But if you wish to be daring, here are a few expressions that may help you:

please cut it	bitte schneiden
on the sides	an den Seiten
in back	hinten
I would like an upsweep	ich hätte es gern hochgesteckt
the bangs	der Pony (short "o")
longer in back	hinten länger
full on the sides	die Seiten voll
too high, curly, straight	zu hoch, kraus, glatt
the permanent	die Dauerwelle
the set	die Wasserwelle, das Einlegen
to dye, to tint	färben, tönen
tease	toupieren
to comb	kämmen

Before putting up your hair, the operator asks, "Möchten Sie Haarfestiger?" (Should I use wave set?) Then she rolls it up on rollers (Lockenwickler) and puts you under the dryer (die Haube). "Möchten Sie etwas lesen?" (Do you want something to read?) she will ask you. "Ja, bitte!" (Yes, please) you will answer and she will bring you a few magazines to kill the time.

Finally comes the time to pay for your new creation. Cutting, wave set, hair spray and so forth will be considered extras and added to the basic price for washing and setting.

Before you leave don't forget to give a tip to the girl who did your hair. The owner of the salon is never tipped.

And here are a few expressions for the benefit of our male readers if they wish to

What Time Is It?

How do you ask for the time? You can ask "Wie spät ist es?" or "Wieviel Uhr ist es?"

Here are some examples of telling time in German:

9:30 = halb zehn

7:45 = viertel vor acht
or: dreiviertel acht

11:05 = fünf nach elf

3:50 = zehn vor vier

8:15 = viertel nach acht
or: ein Viertel neun

10 a.m. = zehn Uhr morgens

10 p.m. = zehn Uhr abends

This is the colloquial usage. In official language, on the radio, or wherever it is important to avoid misunderstandings, one uses the figures 13 (dreizehn) to 24 (vierundzwanzig) for the afternoon hours. For 8:15 p. m., the radio announcer will say "Es ist jetzt zwanzig Uhr fünfzehn." For five minutes past midnight, he would say "Null Uhr fünf," literally: zero hour five.

And note for longer periods: The phrase "a week from today" can be expressed either as "heute in einer Woche" or "heute in acht Tagen." The Germans only count the day of the utterance for a single week (8 days), not for two weeks, which is expressed "in 14 Tagen" or "in zwei Wochen."

(Beware: if someone asks you "Haben Sie Zeit?" or "Hast Du Zeit?" he is not asking for the time but is inquiring if you have time to spend with him!)

Barber Shop (contd.)

have their hair cut in a German barber shop:

normal haircut, tapered back — Fasson

square back — Rundschnitt

trim the ends — Spitzen abschneiden

trim — ausputzen

shortened on top — oben etwas kürzer.

"Entschuldigen Sie, können Sie mir bitte sagen, wie spät es ist?"

Reading and Writing German Figures

The way German figures are written often is confusing for newcomers to Germany. To Americans, the German numeral "one" may look like an American "seven" and the "seven" has a slight resemblance to a capital "F," as it has its stem crossed.

Another difference when reading German figures: the period separates billions, millions, thousands and hundreds, while the comma sets off the decimal fraction.

American usage: US $ 10,000.50
German usage: DM 10.000,50

When the numbers get bigger than a million the vocabulary gets confusing: an American million equals a German one but an American billion (= "Milliarde" in German) is 1,000 times smaller than a German "Billion" (= American trillion).

Dates, too, are written differently: first the day, then the month, and finally the year, with no comma in-between: 20. November 1980 = 20. 11. 1980 (Beware of this trap when filling in German forms!)

In case you are confused: six eggs cost DM 1,70 here.

First Names and Family Names

Christian, Michael, Alexander, Stefan, Andreas, Daniel, Markus, Thomas, Matthias, and Tobias were the most popular names German parents gave their newly-born sons at the beginning of the 1980s. With daughters, it was Christine or Christiane, Stefanie, Nicole, Melanie, Maria, Sandra, Kathrin, Daniela, Nadine; or Julia.

The fashions of first names given change almost as quickly nowadays as the dress fashions. Besides the "hits," other popular names at present include Jakob, Ulrich, Rainer, and Armin with the boys and Barbara, Anne, Vera, Verena, Ursula, and Brigitte with the girls.

Chancellor Schmidt bears the second-most frequent family name in Germany; it is surpassed only by Müller: every hundredth German is named Müller. Other very frequent family names include Meier (Maier, Meyer), Schneider, Fischer, Weber, Bauer, Schäfer, and Klein.

Don't Be Frustrated by the Dialects

Many an American who came to Germany with what he thought a good command of German got the shock of his life once a German started to speak to him. Not understanding a word, he wondered what kind of language he had actually learned at school. Maybe he came to a small town in Bavaria, Swabia, the Palatinate, or Hesse. In those southern and central parts of Germany, local dialects are sometimes especially difficult to understand for foreigners — even for North Germans. Plattdeutsch, still spoken in rural areas of Lower Saxony, Westphalia and Schleswig-Holstein and in the ports, is closer to English but chances are it throws the stranger just as well.

The German spoken in Hannover is generally considered to be the best High-German. However, educated people all over the country are able to speak High-German (although often with a shade of the local dialect), and practically everybody can understand it. And slowly, the foreigner will learn to understand the dialect, too. No reason for frustration!

Foreign Tongues

Every third adult German (and 99 % of the university students and faculty members) speaks a second language in addition to his own. 29 % speak English, 14 % French, but only 1 % Spanish or Italian.

A "Metzger" Is a "Fleischer "

In Hamburg, a butcher is called "Schlachter," in Berlin "Schlächter," but in southern and western Germany the same profession is know as "Metzger," in central Germany as "Fleischer" and in the south-east as "Fleischhacker" or sometimes as "Selcher."

Similarly, a plumber or tin-smith is called "Klempner" in most areas but in the south, "Spengler."

There also exist various names for cleaning woman: Putzfrau, Reinmachefrau, Zugehfrau, Perle ("gem") or, very sophisticated, "Raumpflegerin."

The best example for differences in food names is the roll: "Brötchen" is the most generally accepted term, but you also find "Semmel" or "Weck" (South Germany), "Schrippe" (Berlin), or "Rundstück" (Hamburg).

The Old Towns

On reading your Baedecker on German cities, you will find that many were once a "Free City." What does this mean?

In the old German Empire, these cities (for instance, Augsburg, Nürnberg, Frankfurt, Regensburg, Ulm) were not subject to the prince ruling the region surrounding them but responsible to the Emperor alone. All Free Cities developed a rich tradition of trade and craftsmanship and created a great deal of early German culture.

Only two of the fifty-one Free Cities have remained independent to this day — the city states of Hamburg and Bremen. They and Lübeck (which, however, is today part of the state of Schleswig-Holstein) also retained the by-name of "Hansestadt."

In the 13th to 15th centuries, the "Hanse" was a kind of North-European Common Market, a league of some 160 free trading cities, primarily of northern and central Germany, with branches from London, England, to Nowgorod, Russia.

Many towns in the South and West of Germany originated in Roman times.

A nearby castle (Burg) often gave the town its name (Hamburg, Augsburg).

The Origin of Town Names

Germany still is a picture book of history — at least for those who can read it. Take the names of the towns, for instance: if you know a little bit about their origin, you will look at the places with different eyes. Many town names go back to Roman and Germanic times.

Did you notice that very many town names in Southern Germany end with **-heim** (Mannheim, Rosenheim)? Historians say this shows that they were once founded by Frankish settlers.

The ending syllable **-furt** (as in Frankfurt or Schweinfurt) means that the town originated at a ford, where a river could be passed by wading.

If German town names end or begin with **-reuth, -reut, -reute, -rode, -rod** or **-rath** (as Bayreuth, Osterode or Reutlingen), this points to the fact that they originated in a wooded area that had to be cleared ("ro-den" in German) of trees and their stumps before houses could be built and fields could be made arable.

Many towns in Southern and Western Germany originated from Roman settlements in the first centuries A.D. All names ending in **-weiler, -weier, -wihl** or **-weil** (as Appenweier or Rottweil) developed from the Latin word "villa," just as **-kastel** (as in Bernkastel) goes back to the Latin "castellum" (castle).

If a name ends with **-burg** (as Hamburg or Augsburg), this shows that the town sprung up near or around a Burg, a castle.

Towns originating around abbeys, convents, etc. often still carry the word **Kloster** or **Mönch** (= monk) in their names (Klosterreichenbach, München). A name containing **-zell** (Mariazell) points to the cell of a hermit.

Town names ending with **-ingen** (Sigmaringen) usually lie in Swabia, those with **-ing** (Dingolfing) in Bavaria. The name Sigmaringen tells that the settlement was founded by a Teuton called Sigmar and his kin.

Berlin, Germany

"We went to Munich, Germany, and then to Brussels, Belgium, and on to Madrid, Spain," an American tourist would say in describing his European travels; from the huge U.S.A. he is used to adding the state to the city name. Not so the European. Normally, he would not add the countries' names in this case. Nor would a German add the federal state's name (Rheinland-Pfalz, Hesse, Bavaria) to the city, as hardly any misunderstandings are possible. "Ich komme aus Köln und will nach Mannheim," he would just say.

Something on Proverbs

Germans and Americans have many proverbs in common, although the pictures they use are not always the same. It is interesting to compare some:

German	American
Ein Spatz in der Hand ist besser als die Taube auf dem Dach. (A sparrow in the hand is better than a dove on the roof)	A bird in the hand is worth two in the bush.
Wer andern eine Grube gräbt, fällt selbst hinein. (He who digs a trap for others will fall into it himself)	He that mischief hatcheth, mischief catcheth.
Wo gehobelt wird, fallen Späne. (Where one planes, there will be shavings)	You cannot make an omelette without breaking eggs.
Vom Regen in die Traufe. (From the rain into the gutter)	From the frying pan into the fire.
Der Apfel fällt nicht weit vom Stamm. (The apple does not fall far from the tree)	A chip off the old block.
Wenn man den Wolf nennt, kommt er gerennt. (If you name the wolfe, he comes running)	Speak of the devil, and he is sure to appear.
Aus einer Mücke einen Elefanten machen. (To make an elephant out of a mosquito)	To make a mountain out of a molehill.

"Der Apfel fällt nicht weit vom Stamm" — a chip off the old block.

Shopping in Germany

For foreigners not speaking German and not knowing their way around yet, the large department stores offer the easiest shopping opportunities to start with. They look pretty much the same all over the Western World now, and you can browse to your heart's content practically without having to speak to a salesperson.

It's different in the smaller shops and boutiques, but you shouldn't avoid them for fear of having to speak because you might miss an opportunity to get in touch with the "real Germany" that you had wanted to meet ever since coming over. Besides, many salespersons do speak a little English.

A Few Tips

It's customary to say "Guten Tag" when entering a small shop and "Auf Wiedersehen" when leaving. When you are approached by a salesperson and you're not ready to buy something yet, say "ich möchte mich nur umsehen" (I just want to look around). Ample use of "bitte" (please) and "danke" (thank you) is never wrong!

Footwear and clothing you should always try on (anprobieren) as not only the sizes vary but also the cuts, and there are additional variations between products from various countries — France, Italy, Greece, Spain, East European or Far East countries. The exchange of items bought is called "Umtausch."

Look for "Sonderangebot" and "Sonderpreis" (reduced prices) but beware of the large price signs that show the word "ab" before the price: "Hemden ab 10.-." This means "and up," and usually there will be just a very few shirts at 10.- available and all the others are "and up." Therefore, always read the individual price tag, too.

Souvenir items you should buy in big German stores, not at the souvenir stands where the quality and selection usually is not so good and the prices are higher.

Supermarkets

German supermarkets operate pretty much the same as those elsewhere, except that the products are named differently and the weights are metric. Meat is cut differently, and this, we're afraid, is something that you can only learn by trying what is offered here.

Even in the largest supermarkets there will be no "bagger" to pack your groceries and carry them out to your car. Wages are just too high in Germany for such "luxury," so you'll have to be your own bagger. In many places you can use the same cart with which you took the merchandise to the cashier to transport them to the parking lot. Generally plastic — not brown paper — bags are available but as a result of rising oil prices they often cost a bit extra (usually ten Pfennigs).

Credit Cards, Charge Accounts

Germans usually pay everything in cash or, in the case of larger sums, with the popular "eurocheque" (see page 31). Many shops and restaurants accept cards from Diners Club, American Express, Carte Blanche and Eurocard, but on the whole credit cards are not used very much in Germany. Europeans are always struck by the bundles of credit cards some Americans are carrying around.

Instalment buying is well known here, too, particularly for cars and furniture. With very few exceptions, department stores do not offer charge accounts in Germany.

No State Taxes

When you see a price tag in a German store you can be sure that it shows the final price, all taxes included. There are no special state taxes or sales taxes that might be added.

In the last decades, thousands of small shops have given way to the large supermarkets and department stores. Those which remained often stick out for specialties, high quality, and personalized service.

Thrift Mentality

Foreigners sometimes wonder how the average German wage-earner makes ends meet in view of the high prices in Germany. The answer lies in a certain "thrift mentality."

Most Germans shop very carefully, always comparing prices and taking advantage of special offers or sales. When buying more expensive items they usually look for high, durable quality.

Do-it-yourself repairing is highly popular, as is "Schwarzarbeit" (black work), i.e. illicit side-line work, such as painting jobs, which is much cheaper because no taxes and social security contributions are included in the price.

Generally, the average German also tries to avoid the costs of being indebted — unless unavoidable, like when buying a house or apartment. Putting money into savings accounts is still wide-spread, although social security protects everyone against dire need caused by unemployment, sickness, and old age.

Overcome the Measuring Barrier!

There is much talk of the language barrier separating Americans from their European surroundings. What many forget is another barrier, just as frustrating, but much easier to overcome — the measuring barrier.

You're in the middle of Frau Schmidt's favorite cookie recipe, and are stopped short by the notation "150 grams flour."

A German friend tells you in horror that it was 38 degrees during his Italian vacation and you don't know whether he sweltered or froze.

Your car needs 10 gallons of gas and the attendant asks, "How many liters, please?"

While the U. S. is slowly, gradually switching over to the metric system and many goods are now already labeled both in the old and in the metric units to make the transition easier, Americans coming to Europe are plunged head-over into a metric world, which can be quite confusing for someone used to living with feet and inches, ounces and gallons.

Think Metric!

Living in Europe is a lot simpler for the American who "thinks metric" from the start. He can go into any store and order with authority, without depending on some helpful sales clerk or fellow buyer who will convert for him.

If you start out with two basic facts, you'll do fine with the metric system from the beginning. First, remember that measurements are based on 100, not all kinds of numbers like 16 ounces to a pound, or 5,280 feet in a mile. Second, the prefix "centi" means hundredth; "kilo" means thousand.

Thus, a meter has 100 centimeters; a kilometer has 1,000 meters. Similarly, a kilogram has 1,000 grams, a liter 100 centiliters, and so on.

As we said, it's much better to start thinking metrically instead of always converting from American measurements, but one has to start, of course, from comparisons:

A meter is about 39 inches;
a kilogram, or kilo, is 2.2 pounds;
a liter is 2.113 pints;
a kilometer is 5/8 of a mile.

For practical purposes, though, you don't have to be so exact. Supposing you want to buy some yardage for a dress. Since a meter is slightly more than a yard, you know you'll have some left over if you order four meters when the pattern calls for four yards.

Or you need 10 gallons of gas. Since there are about four liters in a gallon, you'll buy 40 liters.

Shopping for food, you have another help, because many Germans still commonly measure by the Pfund, or pound. A Pfund is a half kilo, or 500 grams. This makes it just slightly more than the U.S. pound (454 grams).

Ein Achtel Wurst

A delight to the housewife with a small family is the German custom of selling foods in very small quantities. If you want just enough brussels sprouts to feed two people, order ein halbes Pfund (half pound) and the clerk will measure and wrap it as politely and painstakingly as if you had ordered two kilos.

Or if you'd like to serve a large variety of cheese and sausages, you can order them by the quarter or even eighth of a pound. A quarter pound is ein Viertel; an eighth of a pound, ein Achtel.

Milk, cream, wine and other liquids are measured by the liter — a little over a quart.

When it comes to recipes, things are not so easy. Germans are not used to measuring cups and spoons, but use scales instead. This is a much more exact system, which eliminates such American complications as sifting flour before measuring it. A hundred grams of flour, after all, weigh 100 grams, sifted or not.

You won't be far off, however, if you estimate a cup of sugar as 200 grams; a cup of flour, 150 grams; a teaspoonful, 5 grams, a tablespoonful, 12 grams.

German recipes are, in any case, much less precise than American ones. They commonly require that one "brown the meat, add some onions, some tomato paste and some flour and then water and spices and cook until tender." The rest is left to the cook's imagination.

Shopping for clothes is probably the least of your problems. If the purchase is for you, the salesperson can easily estimate your size. Many large department stores have conversion tables of American and German sizes, and most salespeople who commonly wait on Americans know these by heart.

The conversion table at the end of this booklet will help you with dresses, shoes, shirts, etc. Stocking sizes in Germany are the same as in America.

But we still haven't found out if our German friend sweltered or froze during his Italian vacation. Well, to begin with, 32 degrees Fahrenheit, or freezing, is 0 degrees Centigrade. To figure out all other temperatures, simply take the centigrade reading, multiply by 9, divide by 5 and add 32. So, now do you know?

Carlotta Anderson

Think Metric!

Ordering a quarter (ein Viertel) pound of cold cuts is not uncommon in Germany.

A kilometer is a little more than half a mile, 10 kilometers are 6 miles.

Thirty degrees Centigrade mean a hot day.

Buying Clothes and Shoes

"Bitte sehr?" the sales girl (die Verkäuferin) in the clothes shop asks the lady customer (die Kundin). What do you wish to buy — ein Kleid (dress), eine Bluse (blouse), einen Rock (skirt), ein Kostüm (suit), or einen Mantel (coat)? A pullover is also called "Pullover" in German, but with the stress on the second syllable, or "Pulli" in short. A "Wolljacke" or "Weste" is a cardigan.

"Welche Größe haben Sie?" (what size do you wear?) is the next question. Know the German sizes? To get the German sizes, add 8 to the U. S. sizes for blouses, 28 to those for skirts, dresses and coats, and 31 to those for shoes. For example, if you wear a size 14 dress in the States, you'll take a German size 42. "Wollen Sie es anprobieren?" (Do you wish to try it on?)

"Ich möchte ein Paar schwarze Schuhe, Größe 43, bitte" (I want a pair of black shoes, size 12, please!) Some more terms that you might need: "zu eng" — too narrow; "zu weit" — too wide; "zu spitz" — too pointed; "zu breit" — too broad. (For the ladies: high heels are "hohe Absätze" in German, medium heels — "halbhohe Absätze," flat heels — "flache Absätze").

Buying Food in German Stores

For the benefit of American housewives living on the German economy, we furnish here a list of words you may find helpful to know when buying food in Germany.

Although the U.S. type of supermarket is becoming increasingly popular in Germany, too, the old-fashioned specialized store is still here.

Such "Läden" (stores, the singular is "der Laden") or "Geschäfte" include:

die Bäckerei (bakery)

die Konditorei (pastry/confectioner's shop)

die Metzgerei or Fleischerei or Schlachterei (butcher's shop)

Quite often, a sign outside these shops says what kind of commodity they sell. For instance:

Brot (bread), Milch (milk), Fleisch (meat), Obst und Gemüse (fruit and vegetables), Wein und Spirituosen (wines and liquors), Kaffee, Tee, Schokolade (coffee, tea, chocolate), Fische (fish).

"Kolonialwaren" (originally "colonial products") means grocery store, as does "Feinkost," but the latter is closer to Delikatessen. "Lebensmittel" stands for grocery store.

Grocery stores often are recognizable by signs of certain co-operative associations or chains they belong to. Examples for such names are Konsum (Produktion in Hamburg), Edeka, Spar, Ve-Ge, VIVO, Rewe, etc. Self-Service is "Selbstbedienung" in German.

When entering a German shop, it is always correct to say "Guten Tag" or, if it is before noon, "Guten Morgen." In Southern Germany, many people greet each other with "Grüss' Gott." If a salesgirl (die Verkäuferin) asks you what you want, she will probably say "Bitte schön?" or just "Bitte?" or "Werden Sie schon bedient?" or "Bekommen Sie schon?" (Are you being attended to?)

Now you may either say "Ich möchte gern..." or "Ich hätte gern..." (I would like...) or you may also spare this introduction and say right away what you want. To be able to do this, there is one thing you must learn by all means: the German figures from one to hundred. You need this not only for ordering sechs Brötchen or vier Zitronen (six rolls or four lemons) but also for paying.

As to the things you want to buy, we cannot list all the commodities here that you may wish to get, but we will give some examples showing how to use the most important quantity terms:

ein Brot
a loaf of bread

ein Paket Schwarzbrot
a package of (black) rye bread

ein halber Liter Milch
a little over a pint of milk

ein Pfund or ein halbes Kilo Butter
one pound (500 grams, i. e. almost 2 oz. more than 1 lb.) of butter

ein viertel Pfund Käse
a quarter pound (125 grams) of cheese

zwei Stück Torte
two pieces of fancy cake

ein Becher Schlagsahne
a cup of whipped cream

hundert Gramm Keks
100 grams (approx. 3 1/2 oz.) of cookies

vier Würstchen
four frankfurters

ein Kopf Salat
a head of lettuce

eine Dose Orangensaft
a can of orange juice

eine Flasche Wein
a bottle of wine.

To understand the prices, you also ought to know these abbreviations:

l = Liter (a little over a quart)

kg = Kilo (1,000 grams, a little more than two lbs.)

g or gr = Gramm (15,4 grains)

The Money

When it comes to paying, the shopgirl may ask you: "Haben Sie Kleingeld?" or "Haben Sie's klein?" (Do you have coins?). If you don't, you may say: "Leider nicht, ich habe nur einen Zehn- (Zwanzig-, Fünfzig-, Hundert-) Markschein!" (Sorry no, I only have a 10- (20, 50, 100) Mark bill).

There are eight different coins in German money, i. e. ein Pfennig, zwei Pfennig, fünf Pfennig, zehn Pfennig (called ein Groschen), fünfzig Pfennig, eine Mark, zwei Mark and fünf Mark. In banknotes, there are: fünf Mark, zehn Mark, zwanzig Mark, fünfzig Mark, hundert Mark and fünfhundert Mark and tausend Mark bills.

Litfaßsäule

Everywhere in German streets you will see big round columns covered all over with posters. They are called "Anschlagsäulen" (advertising pillars) or "Litfaßsäulen," named after the Berlin printer, Ernst Litfaß, who created the first such pillars in Berlin in 1855. West Berlin alone has over 2,000 of these columns.

Shops Close Early

Americans intending to buy in German stores often are confused and irritated by the early hours at which German shops close their doors. The shop owners are obliged to do so on account of a Federal law which was passed in 1956 in order to protect the interests of small shop-keepers and shop personnel. Criticism against this law is growing, however, and many Germans, especially working house-wives, hope that it will be modified one day.

In Germany, all shops, with some exceptions, are obliged by law to close Monday through Friday from 6:30 p.m. until 7 a.m. the following day and at 2 p.m. Saturday. On every first Saturday in the month and on the four Saturdays before Christmas shops can be kept open until 6 p.m. Within these limits, shop owners can fix their individual opening and closing hours. In villages and small towns, as well as in the suburbs of bigger cities, most stores close for an hour or so around noontime.

Stands selling fruit, candy, newspapers and similar articles at the federal German railway stations can be kept open all day long and throughout the night.

Outside the hours fixed for all other shops, however, they are supposed to sell only to customers using the trains, but this law is often bypassed. Other exceptions from the rule were introduced for tourist spots during the season, when shops may be open all day on Saturday and also on Sunday afternoons.

The law allows certain shops to open also on Sundays. The hours differ in the various states. Milk shops may be open on Sunday mornings; flower shops around noon; and bakery shops, selling their own cakes, in the early afternoon. Newspapers can be sold from 11 a.m. until 1 p.m. (sometimes also in the morning) on Sundays und from 6 a.m. until 7 p.m. every weekday.

Shops must close at 6.30 p.m. Monday through Friday.

Sales Twice a Year

Twice a year, two weeks in winter and in summer (starting officially on the last Monday in January and the last Monday in July respectively), German shops have their big sales, called "Winter-" or "Sommerschlussverkauf" or, more popular, "Ausverkauf." Of late, many shops have begun with "Ausverkauf" much earlier than on the fixed dates, offering certain items at reduced prices as "Sonderangebot" (special offer). For instance, buying warm clothes right after Christmas may be a good idea.

"Schlußverkauf" means sales.

"Handeln"

Haggling ("handeln") is regarded as sort of demeaning in Germany and in northern Europe in general. It just isn't done, or rarely done, to put it correctly. You may try your bargaining talents at a flea market, for instance, or when buying a second-hand car — but don't count on it.

The Open Markets

Buying at the "Markt" is highly popular in Germany

Regularly on market days (once or twice a week), summer and winter, outdoor markets are held all over Germany, in small towns as well as in big cities. Everywhere on the market places one can see the heavily laden counters of eggs, salami and cheese, the tables piled high with fruit and vegetables, the stands selling fish and meat, flowers and household utensils, inexpensive books and clothes. There is always a bustling, lively atmosphere about these markets, with the dealers crying their wares, enticing the swarming buyers to buy from their goods and not that of their neighbor.

The "Markt" in modern Europe is to be seen today practically as it was many centuries ago. So if it's a bargain you want and a little bit of "Old Europe," then the market place is a must.

Probably because of their personalized atmosphere, the open markets have grown in popularity in Germany, especially if they are held amidst shopping districts and near modern supermarkets. Two thirds of all German housewives like to buy at the street market if they have the opportunity.

Local authorities, by the way, supervise these markets and see to it that the sanitary regulations are observed.

Drogerie Is Not Drugstore

A German "Drogerie" is not quite the same as an American "drugstore." A Drogerie will sell toiletries, household cleansers, babyfood, camera supplies, wallpaper, seeds, paints, etc. but it does not deal in prescription medicine, and you will not be able to get something to eat there.

Parfümerie

A "Parfümerie" sells cosmetics, perfumes, soaps, etc.

Apotheke

An "Apotheke" (pharmacy) sells medicine with and without prescriptions, and also some toilet articles.

Reformhaus

A "Reformhaus" is comparable with an American Health or Natural Food Store. It sells special foods, teas and vitamins, always with an eye toward health.

A "Drogerie" sells many things, but not food or drinks.

Folk Festivals, Holiday Customs,
Leisure Time Pursuits

Meet Merry People

A great number of folk festivals take place in Germany every year. Preserved from olden days, when the individual regions of the country still had little contact with the outside world, festivals developed according to the particular customs of the area. These folk festivals always meet with great interest not only on the part of the German population but also on the part of foreign visitors.

World-famous, of course, is the Munich Oktoberfest. Other more intimate events, however, certainly are no less attractive. Some of these include the "Shepherds' Dance" in Rothenburg ob der Tauber, the "Kinderzeche" in Dinkelsbühl, the "Fishermen's Jousting" in Ulm, the "Goat Auction" in Deidesheim and the "Shepherds' Run" in Markgröningen and Urach. These are just a few of the more well known historical folk festivals.

Wine Festivals

In the late summer and in autumn, wine festivals are celebrated in all wine growing regions: on the Rhine, in the Palatinate, on the Moselle, Nahe, Ruwer and Saar rivers, in the Eifel area, along the "Mountain Road" between Heidelberg and Darmstadt, in Baden, Württemberg, at Lake Constance and in Franconia. The first wine festivals take place as early as June, but the season really begins in September, with the wine harvesting season.

Attending a wine festival, expecially in a small place, can be a rewarding experience. Here one meets the people whose daily work and life are centered around the cultivation of wine. One feels how it determines the rhythm of their lives, how diligently and carefully they work for it, and how happily they celebrate the fruit of their labor.

The largest German wine festival, which dates back to the year 1442, is held annually in Bad Dürkheim in the Palatinate, which is Germany's largest wine growing community. The festival is called "Wurstmarkt" (Sausage Fair) and attracts more than 500,000 visitors from West Germany and the neighboring countries of Western Europe. In a recent year, for instance, a total of 50,000 gallons of wine, 783 pigs, 60 calves, 105 head of cattle and 50,000 roast chickens were consumed during the seven days and nights in September. It is hard to say what makes the "Sausage Fair" so attractive. It must have

something to do with the wine which gets people into a happy, sociable mood. As a local poet put it: "The Sausage Fair is a festival where you meet lots of friends you have never seen before in all your life."

Other big wine festivals among the hundreds held every year are in Koblenz, Heppenheim, Mainz, Rüdesheim, Assmannshausen, Bacharach, Trier and Bingen. In Neustadt in the Palatinate every year the German and Palatinate "Wine Queens" are chosen and the new wine is given its name.

Oktoberfest in September

Although called Oktoberfest, most of this gigantic affair takes place during the latter part of September. It ends early in October. It really is the Bavarian National Festival and as such the emphasis is on drinking Bavarian beer, not wine. Incredible quantities of "Wiesenbier," which is especially strong, are downed every year at the Oktoberfest, together with many tons of pork sausages and roasted chickens, to say nothing of oxen on the spit. Several million visitors attend the festival each year.

The big "fest" begins with the entrance of the proprietors of the beer halls on the

Theresienwiese (or simply: Wies'n) and the tapping of the first cask by the Lord Mayor. On the following day there is the great Trachtenfest parade, with thousands of participants in folk costumes, with bands, floats and decorated beer wagons drawn by the famous brewery horses. The parade winds through Munich's downtown streets and ends on the festival grounds, the Wies'n.

Oktoberfest had its origins a little over 150 year ago, when the Princess Therese of Saxe-Hildburghausen was married to Bavaria's Crown Prince, Ludwig, who later became King Ludwig I. To celebrate the wedding, it was suggested that a horse race be held. This met the king's approval and horsemen from the whole of Bavaria came to take part with 40,000 visitors looking on. The celebration following the race on the next day was such a great success that it was decided that the place be called Theresienwiese in honor of the Princess and that the fest be repeated each year. And thus the Oktoberfest has become what it is today — Europe's biggest folk festival which nobody being in Munich at that time should miss.

Harvest Thanksgiving

Harvest Thanksgiving is celebrated in numerous ways all over rural Germany. The churches hold special services. Harvest wreaths of wheat and colorful ribbons are a traditional feature. It is not a legal holiday in Germany, however, and not celebrated in the family with such traditional foods as cranberry sauce and pumpkin pie.

In some areas, these festivities fall together with "Allerweltskirchweih" on the third Sunday in October.

Kirchweih

"Kirchweih" — also called Kirmes, Kirchtag, Kerb, Kilbe, or simply Jahrmarkt — is an annual event usually observed in small communities that has its historical roots in the church consecration festivities. An annual market often was part of the festival, and gradually amusement fairs developed as a standing and most important feature of the Kirchweih, with merry-go-rounds, shooting galleries, and all kinds of booths and stands.

Karneval, Fasching — The Crazy Time

An American coming directly from New York to Mainz or Cologne on Rose Monday might easily believe that the Germans had suddenly gone crazy. In the streets he would see crowds of laughing, singing people, often dancing or swaying arm in arm in crazy costumes and masks. Those days before Ash Wednesday, usually in February, are the climax of the carnival season. Karneval is most enthusiastically celebrated in those parts of Germany where there is a Catholic majority, particularly in the South and along the Rhine.

Today it may seem as if carnival is nothing more than an outburst of gaiety and enjoyment of life before Lent begins. But actually in olden times there was a different meaning behind all this.

The custom springs from pre-Christian roots, having developed from superstitious fears at the change of the seasons, when demons who might win power over man had to be exorcized by noise, lights and conjurings. It was believed that men dressed up as demons and witches, animals or spirits were better able to take up the battle with supernatural powers, to help the spring season overcome the demons of winter. In time the Church condoned the ancient pagan practices by regarding them as a legitimate period of healthy release of merriment before Lent.

Carnival starts punctually at 11 minutes after 11 on the 11th day of the 11th month of the preceding year, but the first preparations take place as early as late summer. Cologne, Mainz and Munich are regarded as the three major "carnival cities" of Germany, and each of the three claims its own style of playing the fool under the scepter of Prince Carnival.

Cologne "Karneval"

Cologne prides itself on the fact that its best carnival talent comes from the narrow streets and alleys of the oldest parts of the city. In January and February, the many carnival societies hold dozens of Sitzungen (meetings) with plenty of drinking, singing, schunkeln (swaying arm in arm) and laughing. Odd folk characters appear, tell their funny stories in broad dialect and sing their songs. In the middle of January, "Prince Carnival" is proclaimed in a merry ceremony in which the mayor invests the elected "Prince" with sovereignty over the city. Cologne has no "Princess Carnival" like other cities but, instead, the Kölnischer Bauer (the Peasant of Cologne) and the Kölnische Jungfrau (the Virgin of Cologne).

The latter is always a man — a relic of the old times when the fair sex was excluded from carnival altogether. Only on one day were women admitted to the merry-making, and to this day the Thursday of the week before Ash Wednesday is reserved for Weiberfastnacht (Women's Carnival). Then the women reign over the city.

This is the beginning of the carnival proper. On Friday and Saturday the big masquerades and fancy-dress balls take place. On Sunday afternoon the various quarters of the city and the schools have their special carnival street parades, which sometimes are even more original than the "official" parade on Rose Monday, which is considered the ultimate climax of the drei tolle Tage (three crazy days). This parade usually is four to five miles long. In slow procession, it winds through the city, with huge floats, horses, bands, funny groups of jesters wearing grotesque or comical masks, and "regiments" of the Fools Guilds in their traditional picturesque uniforms. Dense crowds line the streets, and people laugh, drink (mostly it's rather cold), sing, flirt, gape, scream, try to catch the candy that rains down from the floats... Rich and poor, high and low, learned and simple — they all are just one big, crazy family. The city is turned upside down, and normal business is practically at a standstill.

Mainz Fassenacht

Carnival in the other Rhineland cities follows very much the same pattern, with local variations, of course. The Mainz variety, called Fassenacht, is considered by many to be the most distinguished in Germany. Especially renowned is the quality of the carnival Sitzungen in Mainz. Also, the Mainzers have an unusual number of very picturesque "Guards" in their big Rose Monday parade, wearing historical uniforms. All in all, their carnival seems to be more gemütlich than in other cities; there is an atmosphere of genuine, friendly merriness all over the place.

Munich Fasching

Munich, where carnival is called Fasching, boasts an old traditional carnival spirit born of more southerly, more light-hearted regions. By way of Vienna, the splendor of the Venetian carnival has had an influence on the innumerable balls that take place at this time of the year.

A very old feature of Munich's fasching is the "Dance of the Coopers" which is presented only every seven years in the streets of the city. It originated in the Middle Ages, after the plague had swept the country. The coopers were the first courageous ones to go out into the streets and with all kinds of dances and merry-making tried to get people out of their houses again.

Of course, carnival is not limited to the big cities alone; throughout Bavaria and the Rhineland, even the smallest villages compete with each other in arranging car-nival processions and setting up princes of their own. Each region has its own carnival "war cries." In the Rhineland it's "Helau" or "Alaaf," while Munich responds with "Eins, zwei, g'suffa," which is a frank avowal of the role that drinking plays in the merry-making of fasching.

Swabian Fasnet

Something rather special is carnival in Swabia, where it is called Fasnet. Traces of ancient Germanic cult practices are to be found much more clearly here than in other regions.

Members of the Fools Guilds, masked grotesquely, sway and weave through the streets in the traditional Narrensprung, a remnant of the ancient pre-Christian priests' ritual. There is Federhannes, with a feathered headdress, and Schantele, whose mask depicts half sadness, half joy and who hops along in rhythm to the music with his walking stick and umbrella. Most striking, though, are the Gschell-Narren who carry 40 pound sets of bells around their necks. Their masks show huge, gaping mouths with teeth, and the bells make a deafening noise.

These customs are best preserved in Rottweil, a little town on the Neckar river, but many other towns and villages in the region observe carnival time in very much the same fashion.

But wherever it may be — at midnight Tuesday, when Lent begins, the days of exuberant joyfulness find a sudden, almost dramatic end.

No "Grabbing for Checks"

A word of advice in case you attend a folk-festival for the first time: generally, there is little "treating." Each orders and pays for his own beer and food. If a German should offer to buy you a beer, accept with thanks, then later on reciprocate. There is no "grabbing for checks," however.

Richtfest

Wherever a new building is erected in Germany, a special celebration, the "Richtfest," is held when the roof's framework is raised. A wreath of pine branches, decorated with colored ribbons, is placed atop the roof. Then the chief carpenter climbs up and delivers a speech in poetry before the workers, the architect, the future occupants and their guests, expressing joy over the completed work and asking God's blessing on the house. He drinks a glass of wine and, to bring good luck, smashes the glass on the structure.

Afterwards, all assemble in a half-completed room of the new house or in a tavern for more drinking and eating, plus more speeches.

The picturesque black costume of the journeymen carpenters is an old tradition. They wear bell-bottomed corduroy pants, matching vest and jacket with mother-of-pearl buttons and a floppy, wide-brimmed hat, sometimes one gold earring.

In many places a decorated bush, looking almost like a Christmas tree, takes the place of the wreath.

A wreath of pine branches decorated with colored ribbons shows that the completion of the roof framework has been celebrated.

Journeymen carpenters still wear the traditional black corduroy costumes.

"Laternegehen"

During the first weeks of fall, when the evenings are getting longer, you can sometimes see groups of children carrying candle-lit bright paper lanterns through the streets as they sing of the sun, moon and stars. Mostly they just walk along with mother, but some towns arrange big lantern parades. This is a fall custom primarily in Northern Germany, while the St. Martin's lantern parades in November take place in the predominantly Catholic West and South of the country.

For more details on German holidays and the customs connected with them, see our booklet "German Holidays and Folk Customs."

Children sing "Sonne, Mond und Sterne" while carrying their paper lanterns through the streets in early fall.

Another nice custom connected with children: The little tots starting school are consoled by their parents on the first day with huge, colorful cardboard cones filled with sweets or small toys.

The Old Costumes

Hessian Folk Customs

Only if you are lucky, and only in rural areas of Germany, particularly in Hessen, Bavaria and the Black Forest, can you still see people wearing the old folk costumes. Nowadays, they wear them only for church, especially on church holidays, and for weddings and similar occasions.

The Chimney Sweep

Another picturesque remnant from olden times is the hat worn by German chimney sweeps ("Schornsteinfeger" or "Kaminkehrer"). Most Germans believe meeting a chimney sweep or even touching him brings them good luck.

Opposite Page:

If you have an opportunity to do some traveling in Germany, you will notice that farm houses, especially older ones, differ greatly from one region to the other. On the opposite page we present six houses typical of various West German regions. Of course, there are many variations of these prototypes.

Hesse/Frankonia

Black Forest

Moselle Valley

Upper Bavaria

Lower Saxony

Palatinate

Wedding Customs

In remote areas, some old wedding customs are still being practiced, but on the whole, "Hochzeit" festivities in the States and in Germany are not very different. Some American customs, such as the big wedding cake, the throwing of confetti or rice, or the wedding march are not part of the German tradition.

However, the custom of "Polterabend" (poltern = to make a loud noise) is very popular here. On the eve of the wedding, friends of the couple go to the bride's house and smash piles of old pottery at the door or under her window. It's an old superstition that the loud noise helps to avert bad luck. To assure future married bliss, the bride is expected to sweep up the broken pieces all by herself.

In Germany, the civil marriage is obligatory. It takes place at the local "Standesamt" (registrar's office) in the presence of two witnesses. The church wedding follows the civil marriage.

On the eve of the wedding: Polterabend.

Bridal "Showers" are unknown here, presents are delivered on Polterabend or on the wedding day itself.

How to Congratulate

"Herzlichen Glückwunsch zum Geburtstag!" is the most accepted and popular form of congratulating a German on his birthday. The first two words, "Herzlichen Glückwunsch," or the plural, "Herzliche Glückwünsche," will fit on almost any occasion if you wish to congratulate someone in German, be it a birthday (Geburtstag), a name-day (Namenstag), an engagement (Verlobung), a wedding (Hochzeit), the birth or christening of a baby (Geburt, Taufe), church confirmation or Communion, or an anniversary (Jubiläum).

Greeting Cards

If you want to write your congratulations, you will probably use a greeting card. It is customary to add not only your name to the printed text but also some personal words, such as "Mit allen guten Wünschen" or "Alles Gute für die Zukunft" or whatever the occasion may suggest.

Popular wishes for Christmas and the New Year include "Fröhliche Weihnachten und ein glückliches Neues Jahr!" or perhaps "Ein frohes Weihnachtsfest und viel Glück (or "alles Gute") zum Neuen Jahr!" More formal would be: "Mit den besten Wünschen zum Jahreswechsel!"

In talking, most people wish each other "Frohes Fest!" on these occasions, also at Easter (Ostern) and Whitsuntide (Pfingsten). But you can also wish "Fröhliche Ostern!" and "Fröhliche Pfingsten!"

Flowers and Presents

On receiving an engagement, wedding, or birth announcement, you should send a card with your congratulation. Unless you have special reasons not to cultivate the contact, we would also suggest sending a nice bouquet of flowers along with your congratulations.

Concerning presents, much depends on the relationship between you and the person to whom you want to give a present. This is the same as in the States. The American customs of bridal showers and baby showers are not known in Germany. Here, you send or bring flowers for the mother and/or a little present for the baby after he is born. Engagement presents are given or sent the day of the engagement. Wedding presents often are delivered at the house while the family is attending the church ceremony or — if you are invited to Polterabend — on the eve of the wedding. Likewise, christening presents are given when the family celebration takes place. If you are not invited to the christening but just asked to "come and see the baby," bring flowers and a little present, too.

Flowers are also brought along when visiting sick people. And what do you wish a sick person? Say "Weiterhin gute Besserung!" or, more formal, "Gute Genesung!"

How to Answer

Last but not least you would perhaps like to know what to answer if a German congratulates you in German. Use any of the various "danke"-forms, like "Vielen Dank," "Herzlichen Dank," or "Vielen, herzlichen Dank," adding, perhaps, "Nett, daß Sie gekommen sind" (nice of you to come) or "Nett, daß Sie daran gedacht haben" (nice of you to think of it).

Christmas Customs

Saint Nicholas Day   **Advent Wreath**   **Real Christmas Candles**

Christmas Customs

The Advent Season

The German Christmas season starts with Advent, which is observed in most homes with the Advent wreath. Made of fir branches entwined with bright red ribbons and crowned with four candles, this wreath is either suspended from the chandelier in the living room or placed upon a table.

Each Sunday the family gathers around the wreath and one candle is lit for each week. On the last Sunday before Christmas all four candles have been lit and shed their mellow light — a prefiguration of the coming of Christ.

Saint Nicholas Day

For German children, on December 6th, Saint Nicholas' Day, "Nikolaus" (St. Nick) with long beard, bishop's miter and staff, comes on a sled drawn by a donkey. Mostly his appearance is left up to the children's imagination, for he comes while they are sleeping. Instead of the stocking, German children place one of their shoes on the window sill on the night of the 6th of December, and lo and behold, the next morning the shoes are filled with goodies.

Christmas Markets

In the weeks before Christmas, Christmas Markets (Weihnachtsmärkte) are held in many towns — a custom which of late has gained in popularity. The "Christkindl-markt" in Nürnberg is particularly famous.

Real Candles

Those who contend that a candle-lighted Christmas tree is not safe will certainly meet with opposition in Germany. Many Germans still prefer a tree with real candles to one electrically illuminated.

To be on the safe side those who use real candles mostly keep a bucket of water in the room — just in case. Of course, real candles should always be placed towards the tip of the limbs. Otherwise the limbs above could catch fire, especially if the tree has become dry. The important thing is always to have someone present while the candles are burning.

The electric lights used in Germany are imitations of white or red candles, not colored or flickering lights as on many US Christmas trees.

Christmas Pastry

Christmas pastry also has a long history. "Lebkuchen" and other sweet cookies of all kinds are still standard features of the family Christmas celebration in Germany. And so are "Christstollen" with raisins, nuts, and candied lemon and orange peels, as well as festive meals, often including roast goose, turkey, or carp.

25th and 26th Are Holidays

Christmas Eve (Heiliger Abend) is the main event in Germany, and both the 25th and 26th of December are national holidays.

Gifts are exchanged on Christmas Eve. The modern counterpart of America's Santa Claus is the German "Weihnachts-mann" (literally: christmas man), in whom the figure of St. Nicholas has merged with older, demonic winter figures such as "Knecht Ruprecht," formerly believed to accompany St. Nicholas. In some South German regions, the "Christkind" (Christ Child, "Kriss Kringle") is the mysterious gift-bringer.

Wishing a Merry Christmas

Germans, too, send Christmas cards. But what kind of message do they send? The greeting most often used is "Fröhliche Weihnachten und ein glückliches Neues Jahr!" (Merry Christmas and a Happy New Year), but there are varieties like "Frohe" or "Gesegnete" (blessed) "Weihnacht," etc. (see page 123).

Chances are that you will find yourself on the morning of the 24th of December still having to buy something. When you leave the shop on this day, the salesgirl will most likely wish you "Frohes Fest!" (literally, Merry Holiday). What do you answer? Just say, "Danke, gleichfalls!" or "Danke, das wünsche ich Ihnen auch!" (Thank you, the same to you).

In Germany, too, it is customary to give Christmas presents or tips to people who helped you the year round, like the mailman, the newspaper boy, the garbage collector, the cleaning woman, etc., but there is no hard and fast rule as to how much to give.

"Fröhliche Weihnachten und ein glückliches Neues Jahr!"

"Frohes Fest!" — and a tip.

More on German Holidays

The Germans observe their "Labor Day" (Tag der Arbeit) on the first of May. Traditional May Day celebrations with maypoles, etc. are still held in many towns and villages on this day. As with most other holidays, however, many of the old customs are slowly disappearing.

Good Friday (Karfreitag) and Easter Monday (Ostermontag) are legal holidays in Germany, and so are Ascension Day (Himmelfahrt) and the Monday after Whitsunday/Pentecost (Pfingsten).

June 17 is oberserved as the "Day of German Unity." It was established in the wake of the 1953 uprising of the population in the DDR ("East Germany").

On the whole, Germans have more holidays than Americans, but no holiday with a fixed date is ever moved to a Friday or Monday. So if such days fall on Sundays, it's just tough luck.

Some religious holidays — Heilige Drei Könige, Fronleichnam, Mariä Himmelfahrt, Allerheiligen, Buß- und Bettag — are legal holidays only in those states where the respective denomination (Catholic or Lutheran) is in the majority.

Easter customs include the coloring of Easter eggs, Easter Rides and fire wheels rolled down from the hills. Easter bonfires still are built in many places.

Green twigs are a symbol of Whitsuntide.

At a Dance

Dancing habits in Germany, as in the States, depend very much on the company and place. While there are practically no rules of etiquette left in jazz cellars and at teenager parties, they are still pretty much observed at more formal occasions. Here's how it's done in Germany:

A man who sees a girl he wants to dance with approaches her table, bows slightly to her, and asks to dance with her ("Darf ich bitten?"). If she is escorted, he must ask the escort for permission ("Gestatten Sie?"). After the dance, he accompanies his partner back to her table, bows slightly and thanks both the girl and her escort.

At more formal social events with dancing, a man is expected to dance not only with his wife or girl friend but also (at least once) with the wives of his friends and colleagues.

The practice of "Abklatschen" (cutting in) is only known at very lively and relaxed German parties.

The formal way of asking for a dance. Dances are in series of two or three. You normally dance all three.

Cutting in (abklatschen) is only done at very lively German parties. At any formal or semi-formal dance, cutting in would be out of place.

Night Spots

German bars and discos do not differ much from similar places in other countries. Prices and types of clientele vary greatly, of course.

Discrimination?

Some disco-type establishments use signs such as "Privat-Club" or "Nur für Mitglieder" (Members Only) to be able to handpick their patrons, especially on busy nights. A few are also known to discriminate against young foreign workers and American soldiers. They say that some of the young foreigners are troublemakers and that their noisy behavior will frighten away the steady German patrons. Often, however, it is hard to say whether the reason for turning away patrons really is discrimination or actual overcrowding. Likewise, it is hard to distinguish between poor service and an intentional slight.

Obvious cases of discrimination of military personnel on national or racial grounds should be reported to the commanders. They will take up action with the disco manager or with the appropriate German authorities which on the whole have proven very cooperative in such cases.

An American military paper gave wise advice to its readers: "Act in a European tavern in the same way you would want a foreign soldier to act in a tavern in your home town."

Leisure Time Activities

How do the Germans spend their leisure time? Opinion pollsters have provided us with some information in this respect, too. The following is based on some recent polls and statistics concerning the Germans' leisure time pursuits:

In the evenings, most people apparently watch TV or read papers or magazines. Entertaining visitors in the home rates third. This apparently depends on the size of the home: the larger the house, the more often guests are welcomed.

Every fourth German regularly visits a neighborhood pub (Stammlokal) for a glass of beer or wine and a chat with friends.

Cultural Activities

Because of its long tradition of particularism and cultural diversity, Germany has always been extremely rich in theaters, opera and concert houses, museums, and libraries, most of which are generously supported by state subsidies. In tiny West Germany alone, there are 300 theaters, 80 symphony orchestras, and 1, 800 museums. Actually, most Germans themselves do not even realize how well off they are in this respect. Every fifth citizen said

he or she had never visited a theater, concert or museum.

The Outdoors

As for outdoor activities, walking, hiking, swimming and gardening are most popular. About one third of the population take car trips once in a while, but two thirds of all families go for a walk (Spazierengehen) regularly on Sundays.

Many Germans still get out their best clothes every Sunday, but there is a strong tendency towards casual wear on holidays, especially among people who are tied to an office desk during the week and happy to get rid of formal clothes on the weekend.

Germans love gardening. More than half of all households call a garden their own. Everywhere you can see the carefully tended plots, often in colonies of "Kleingärten" or "Schrebergärten" with their standardized wooden huts. About half a million garden fans are organized in such associations. But green thumbs are not only active in gardens and backyards. About six out of ten balconies in Germany spot flower plants, while 92 % of households have potted plants.

Other Hobbies

Sports, too, are an important leisure time pursuit, of course (see page 134). Other popular hobbies include collecting (an estimated eight million collectors of all sorts, including four million stamp collectors), choir singing, photography, wireless telegraphy, homing pigeons, etc.

The Young

Young people between 13 and 15 years of age have hardly more free time than their elders. Every third person in this group spends the leisure hours with a "clique" of ten or more, going in for sports, swimming, exchanging records, etc. Of the 16 to 18 year-olds, only 15 % visit a disco occasionally on weekends.

Vacations

More than half of the West-German adult population takes a vacation trip every year, 65 % going by car. There are more than half a million caravan trailers in Western Germany, two thirds of which are used for vacation trips. The rest are put up permanently as a kind of second home away from the city.

Tickets for the Theater

„Bitte zwei Karten zu ... Mark für die Acht-Uhr-Vorstellung!" (Two tickets, please, at ... marks, for the 8 o'clock show / performance) is about what one would say when buying tickets for the movie theater (das Kino), the theater (das Theater) or the opera (die Oper). "Kasse" means box-office. The word for booking in advance is "Vorverkauf."

When buying tickets, one must know the difference in the seats. "Parkett" in German means "orchestra," a "Loge" is a box, "1. or 2. Rang" means first or second balcony, "Balkon" is usually the center part of the first balcony, and "Galerie" is the gallery. "Reihe 7, Platz 10" would mean 7th row, seat No. 10.

Germans, by the way, usually dress up and check their coats at the checkroom (die Garderobe) when visiting a theater, opera or concert.

Admission to movies is only between performances. No children under six are allowed in normal adult showings, and certain age groups are excluded from many other films under the German Youth Protection Law.

"Haben Sie noch Karten für heute abend?"
(Have you any tickets left for tonight?)

Germans dress up for the theater, concert and opera, but not for the movies.

The Weather

Americans shivering in the cold German summers can confirm what scientists have found: It takes most people only seven to nine days to adjust to tropical or dry desert temperatures but it can take several years to build up a tolerance for cold weather.

German weather is similar to the weather in the northern-central United States. There is plenty of rain particularly in the northwestern parts, but the "Tips for Coping with Hamburg's Weather," which an American woman published for the benefit of her compatriots living here, are valid for other German regions as well:

1. Accept the fact that it often rains in Hamburg (a drizzly, damp and continuous rain).

2. Never plan an outdoor event where success depends completely upon good weather. Always have an alternative idea in case of rain.

3. Never cancel plans because of rain or wait until a drizzle stops because you may find yourself postponing for days.

4. Voluntary isolation because of bad weather just makes a gray day grayer.

5. Armed with a rain coat (yellow with a hood!), an umbrella and rain boots, forge ahead — you'll notice Germans are all out in the wet and don't even seem to notice it.

6. Dress warmly — which may mean undershirts for the whole family.

7. Don't consider putting winter clothes into storage before May and then you may need to only pack heavy winter coats and boots.

8. Even sunny days can be cold because of the wind. A wind breaker with a hood (and zip-out warm lining for year-round use) is essential.

9. .Birds awake chirping at 4 a. m., and may bother you in the summer. You'll probably go to work or send your children to school in the dark in winter.

10. Decorate rooms in bright, light colors. Add bright touches to dectract from outside gloom. Use cut flowers and candles.

(From the Handbook of the American Women's Club of Hamburg)

Summer temperatures can get into the 90s — but seldom for more than a few days or weeks. In the winter the temperature is often below freezing. The coldest weather is in the Alps; Germany's warmest area is the Upper Rhine Valley, in the southwest.

The weather is much less extreme in Central Europe than in most parts of the U.S. The moderating influence of the western winds from the Atlantic Ocean is stronger than the hot or cold air streams coming from the eastern land masses. Intense heat is as rare as is extreme cold or blizzards. There are heavy storms at the coasts sometimes but nothing comparable to hurricanes. Earthquakes are practically unknown — apart from a very slight shake once in a while in the southwest or west of the country.

Geographically, Germany lies at the same latitude approximately as southern Canada. Summer days in Germany are longer than in the U.S., winter days are shorter. Summer and winter take long in coming: the spring and fall seasons stretch over longer periods than in more southern countries.

Bathing cabins are rare on German beaches

On the Beach

Northern Germany has fine beach resorts. Bathing attire is about the same as in the States. Very small children, however, often swim and play on the beach naked (even many adults do in some areas).

Beach life German style entails renting a "Strandkorb" ("beach chair") or building for yourself a "Burg" (low circular wall of sand), but it is also usual to sun yourself while lying on a blanket. The "Strandkorb" and the "Burg" protect the bather from the wind.

Since adults don't usually run through the town in beach attire, they must obviously change someplace (bathing cabins are only known at public swimming pools.) It's quite an art to get out of your suit and into your clothes in public with the aid of a protective "Bademantel" (bath robe, usually made from terry cloth). But that's the way it's done. Your neighbors, in the meantime, will discreetly look at the birds passing overhead or at an imaginary steamer in the distance.

The Most Popular Games

If you live in Germany and are looking for an opportunity to come into contact with Germans, joining a sports club may be a good idea: of a total population of some 60 million (in West Germany and West Berlin), some 18 million are organized in 54,000 sports clubs of all sorts.

Soccer

Soccer (Fussball), of course, is the king of sports in Germany — attracting an average of 20 million spectators both to the arenas and TV sets every Saturday afternoon during the Bundesliga season. The big championship matches and the European "Cups" and other international encounters draw up to 70 % of the German population to the TV sets.

The Fussball-Bundesliga (Federal Soccer League) ist the "first division" of German soccer, consisting of the 18 best teams. Every season two to three teams are "demoted" and two to three advance from the second into the first division.

It is not only the dramatic fight for the championship and the just as bitter fight against "demotion" that makes this sport so attractive but also the local patriotism involved, the stardom of the high-paid players and coaches, and — last but not least — the game itself, the rules of which are easy to understand for everybody.

Almost four million West Germans are members of more than 27,000 soccer clubs, but only two million of them are active players.

Other Sports Clubs

Next to soccer, athletics clubs (Turnvereine) have the most members — almost three million. Rifle, track and field, tennis, swimming, handball, and table tennis clubs follow, in that order.

Kegeln

Nine-pin bowling (Kegeln), a bowling game resembling ten-pins played without the headpin, is also very popular: its 1,100 clubs have about 150,000 members, but an estimated three to four million West Germans play it as a hobby without being organized in a club.

U.S.-style bowling, too, has become very popular in Germany in recent decades.

Skat

The number of people playing Skat, the most popular card game in Germany, cannot even be estimated. It is a typical German institution and is played at all levels of society. Even the members of Bonn's parliament have their own club, and a large tavern there organizes a monthly tournament at which journalists and politicians oppose each other. The German military (Bundeswehr), too, organizes its own Skat championship.

Contrary to Fussball, Skat rules are not so easily learned, and it takes a while to learn both the rules and the language of bidding and scoring. Once absorbed, however, it can become a fascinating game.

Soccer, Bowling, and Skat

"Fussball" (soccer) is the most popular sport in Germany, comparable in its popularity only to U. S. baseball and football combined.

"Skat" is by far the most popular card game in Germany. All it takes is three players and a pack of 32 cards — but also a lot of practice.

"Kegeln" (nine-pins) is a bowling game — like ten-pins played without the headpin. Many Germans enjoy the cheerful companionship this game brings about. It makes you thirsty for beer, too!

Volksmarching

"Volksmarsch" (or Volkswanderung, Volkswandertag) is a German word for an organized hike or walk — there's no "marching" on a Volksmarsch, and no competition either. American soldiers stationed in Germany and their families have taken to the idea for several reasons: it's a good way to meet and get to know the German people; it's fun, and you get close to nature; and, finally, it's a healthful activity. Each weekend, an estimated 10,000 to 40,000 Americans participate in the ten-year-old Volksmarch phenomenon.

Usually, a Volksmarsch leads along well marked trails in distances from five to 42 kilometers. Most marches have at least two distances (usually 10 and 20 km) and some have three or four (usually including a marathon hike of 30 km).

Besides improving their health, volksmarchers can also earn awards for each march in the form of certificates, plates, plaques or medals. For continued participation, pins and badges are awarded. Most Volksmarches are sanctioned by one of the organizing groups (IVV, EVG, DLV or DWB) which conduct events throughout the year.

Every Volksmarsch is well publicized in the area. Americans living in a military community should check the local unit or community newspaper or ask unit athletics and recreation officers, local recreation centers, Army Community Service (ACS), or "Kontakt" groups for information. There are also many clubs you can join. Clubs offer a variety of volksmarching benefits, including preregistration.

Volkslauf

A close relative of the volksmarch is the "Volkslauf" (run). Volksläufe are sponsored by the German Track and Field Federation and are timed events. The competition aspect of the Volkslauf is what differentiates it from the volksmarch.

No marching on a "Volksmarsch"

Appendix

The Menu Language

Do you get tired of always ordering Wiener Schnitzel in German restaurants because you don't know how to translate the menu? Here is a handy reference table to make it easy for you to know your way around. Clip it out and keep it in your wallet or purse. Guten Appetit!

Vorspeisen — **Hors d'Oeuvres**

Austern	Oysters
Gänseleberpastete	Paté de foie gras
Krebsschwanzsalat	Crayfish salad
Blätterteigpastete	(flaky) pastry
Räucheraal	Smoked eel
Räucherlachs	Smoked salmon
Russische Eier	Russian eggs
Weinbergschnecken	Snails

Suppen — **Soups**

Erbsensuppe	Pea soup
Gulaschsuppe	Hungarian soup
Hühnerbrühe	Chicken broth
Königinsuppe	Cream of chicken broth
Kraftbrühe	
Linsensuppe	Lentil soup
Nudelsuppe	Noodle soup
Ochsenschwanzsuppe	Oxtail soup
Schildkrötensuppe	Turtle soup
Tomatensuppe	Tomato soup

Salate — **Salads**

Gurkensalat	Cucumber salad
Gemischter Salat	Mixed salad
Kopfsalat	Lettuce salad
Rohkostplatte	Vegetarian salad
Selleriesalat	Celery salad
Tomatensalat	Tomato salad
Salatsoße	Salad dressing

Fische — **Fish**

Aal	Eel
Bodensee-felchen	Snipe (from Lake Constance)
Forelle	Trout
Hecht	Pike
Karpfen	Carp
Makrele	Mackerel
Rheinsalm	Rhine salmon
Schellfisch	Fresh Haddock
Scholle	Plaice
Seezunge	Sole
Steinbutt	Turbot
Zander	Pike-perch
	Jack salmon

Fleisch — **Meat**

Hammel	Mutton
Kalb	Veal
Lamm	Lamb
Rind/Ochsen-	Beef
Schweine-	Pork

Braten	Roast
Filet	Fillet
Frikassee	Fricassee
Haxe	Knuckle
Hirn	Brains
Leber	Liver
Nieren	Kidneys
Ragout	Ragout/Stew
Steak	Beefsteak
Bratwurst	Fried sausage
Eisbein	Pickled pork
Filetsteak	Fillet steak
Rumpsteak	Rumpsteak
Schnitzel à la Holstein	Fillets of veal à la Holstein
Wiener Schnitzel	Fillets of veal à la Viennoise (Breaded veal cutlet)
Schinken	Ham
Soße	Sauce, Gravy

Geflügel — **Poultry**

Ente	Duck
Gans (Gänsebraten)	Goose
Huhn/Hähnchen	Chicken
Küken	Squab chicken

Taube	Pigeon	Karotten	Carrots	Obstsalat	Fruit salad
Truthahn/Puter	Turkey	weiße Rüben	Turnips	Obst, frisches	Fresh fruit

Wild / **Game**

		Rosenkohl	Brussels Sprouts		
Hase	Hare/Rabbit	Rotkraut, -kohl	Red cabbage		
Hirsch	Venison	Spargel	Asparagus	**Gebäck**	**Pastry**
Reh	Roebuck	Weißkraut	White cabbage/Kale	Berliner Pfannkuchen	Berlin doughnuts
Wildschwein	Wild Boar				(Bismarcks)
Keule	Haunch	**Zubereitungsarten**	**Preparation**	Blätterteiggebäck	Puff pastry (turnovers,
Rücken	Saddle	Blau (Fisch)	Blue (fish boiled)		tarts)
		Gebacken	Baked/fried	Obstkuchen	Fruit cake
Eierspeisen	**Egg Dishes**	Gebraten	Roasted/fried	Teegebäck	Tea cakes
		Gefüllt	Stuffed	Torte	Cake with icing
Pfannkuchen	German pancake	Gekocht	Boiled		(very sweet)
Rührei	Scrambled eggs	Geschmort	Braised/stewed	Amerikaner	Special chocolate or
Spiegeleier	Fried eggs	in Backteig	in batter		sugar-covered cookie
Verlorene Eier	Poached eggs	mit Butter	with butter		(named after Americans)
		Paniert	with breadcrumbs		
Beilagen	**Side Order**	mit Remouladen-	with remoulade sauce	Kekse	Cookies
		sauce		Sandkuchen	Pound cake
Bratkartoffeln	Fried potatoes	vom Rost/gegrillt	Grilled, broiled	Toast	Toast
Kartoffelbrei (Püree)	Mashed potatoes	mit Schlagsahne	with whipped cream		
Pommes Frites	french fries				
Reis	Rice	**Kalte Speisen**	**Cold Dishes**	**Alkoholische Getränke**	**Alcoholic Beverages**
Salzkartoffeln	Boiled potatoes	Aufschnitt	Cold cuts		
Spätzle	Spätzle (dumplings)	Kaltes Geflügel	Cold poultry	Bier (hell/dunkel)	Beer (pale/dark)
Knödel	Dumplings	Käseplatte	Assorted cheeses	Bowle	Punch
Leberknödel	Liver dumplings	Schinken	Ham	Liköre/Spirituosen	Liqueurs/spirits (liquors)
		roh/gekocht)	(smoked/boiled)	Rotwein	Red wine
Gemüse	**Vegetables**	Wurst	Cold cuts	Schaumwein	Champagne/Sparkling
					Wine
Blumenkohl	Cauliflower	**Nachtisch**	**Dessert**	Süßwein	Dessert wine
Champignons	Mushrooms			Weinbrand	Brandy
Grüne Bohnen	String beans	Gefrorenes/Eis	Ice cream	Weißwein	White wine
Grüne Erbsen	Green peas	Kompott	Stewed fruit		
Gurken	Cucumbers				

Metric — U.S. Conversion

German Metric		U.S.	
1	Gramm (g)	0.035	ounce
1	Pfund (500 Gramm)	1.1	pounds
1	Kilogramm	2.2	pounds
1	Zentimeter (cm)	0.3937	inch
2.54	Zentimeter	1	inch
1	Meter (m)	3.280	feet
1609.3	Meter	1	mile

Liquid Measure

1	Liter (l)	2.113	pints
1	Liter	1.056	quarts
3.785	Liter	1	gallon

Dry Measure

1	Liter	0.908	quart
1	Dekaliter (10 liters)	1.135	pecks
1	Hektoliter (100 liters)	2.837	bushels

Kitchen Hints

U.S.	Europe
1 cup sugar	200 g
1 cup flour	150 gr.
1 tsp.	5 gr.
1 tbsp.	12 gr.
1 lb.	450 gr.
1 kilo	2.2 lb.

Kilometers — Miles

1	0.6
3	1.8
5	3.1
8	4.9
10	6.2
15	9.3
20	12.4
25	15.5
30	18.6
35	21.7
40	24.8
45	27.9
50	31.0
100	62.1
150	93.1
200	124.2
250	155.2
300	186.4
350	217.4
400	248.5
450	279.5
500	310.6

Thermometer Readings

German thermometers use the centigrade scale. To convert Fahrenheit to centigrade, subtract 32, then multiply by 5 and divide by 9. To convert centigrade to Fahrenheit, multiply by 9, divide by 5 and add 32. Chart below gives approximate conversion.

C	F
38	100.4
35	95
30	86
25	77
21	69.8
10	50
5	41
0	32
—5	23
—10	14
—15	5
—17	1.4
—25	—13
—30	—22

Clothes Sizes U.S. — Europe

Skirts, Dresses, Coats

U. S.	Europe
10	38
12	40
14	42
16	44
18	46
20	48

Suits

U. S.	Europe
36	46
38	48
40	50
42	52
44	54
46	56
48	58

Shirts

U. S.	Europe
14	36
14 1/2	37
15	38
15 1/2	39
16	41
16 1/2	42
17	43

Blouses

U. S.	Europe
30	38
32	40
34	42
36	44
38	46
40	48

Shoes

U. S.	Europe
6	37
7	38
8	39
9	40
10	41
11	42
12	43
13	44

Hats

U. S.	Europe
7	57
7 1/8	58
7 1/4	59
7 3/8	60
7 1/2	61

Here are some tips for easy conversion of U.S. clothes sizes to German sizes:

For blouses, add 8 to your U.S. size to get the German size, for example, if you wear a 34 U.S., you'll take a 42 German. For dresses and skirts you'll have to add 28 to your U.S. size. For shoes, you add 31. For example, size six would become size 37.

Addresses of German National Tourist Offices

U.S.A.:

630 Fifth Avenue
New York, N.Y. 10020
Telephone: (212) 757-8570

104 South Michigan Ave.
Suite 306
Chicago, Ill. 60 603
Telephone: (312) 263-2958

Broadway Plaza, Suite 1714
700 South Flower St.
Los Angeles, Ca. 90017
Telephone: (213) 6 88-73 32

Canada:

P.O. Box 417
47 Fundy, Place Bonaventure
Montreal, Que. H5A 1B8
Telephone: (514) 878-9885

Great Britain:

61, Conduit Street / Regent Street
London W1R OEN
Telephone: 01-734 2600

Index

23Ap84

Other Atlantik-Brücke Publications:

Meet Germany
German Holidays and Folk Customs
Meeting German Business
German Place Names